PHILIP L A

Writer

PHILIP LARKIN
Writer

James Booth

HARVESTER
WHEATSHEAF

New York   London   Toronto   Sydney   Tokyo   Singapore

First published 1992 by
Harvester Wheatsheaf,
66 Wood Lane End, Hemel Hempstead,
Hertfordshire, HP2 4RG
A division of
Simon & Schuster International Group

Typeset in 10/12pt Plantin
by Witwell Limited, Southport

Printed and bound in Great Britain by
Billing & Sons, Worcester

British Library Cataloguing in Publication Data

Booth, James
    Philip Larkin: Writer.
    I. Title
821

ISBN 0-7450-0769-4
ISBN 0-7450-0770-8 pbk

1 2 3 4 5 96 95 94 93 92

CONTENTS

ACKNOWLEDGEMENTS

My thanks are due to Angela Leighton for her rigorous and constructive criticism of succeeding drafts of this book. I am also grateful to Andrew Motion, Jean Hartley, Maeve Brennan, John Howarth and John Riggott for helping me to relate Larkin's life to his writing, and to Janice Rossen and Steve Regan for their advice and encouragement. Various colleagues at the University of Hull have assisted me in different ways, among whom Bruce Woodcock, Marion Shaw, Rowlie Wymer, Owen Knowles, Roger Luckhurst, John Hoyles (English Department), John Osborne (American Studies), Anthony Hedges (Music) and Brian Dyson (Brynmor Jones Library) must be particularly thanked. I am also very grateful to Jenny, Hilda and Eleanor, and to Ruth and Gill for their forbearance.

I would like to thank the Brynmor Jones Library, University of Hull, for permission to quote from Larkin's letters to James Sutton.

Acknowledgement is due to Faber and Faber Ltd. for permission to quote extracts from poems by Philip Larkin originally published in *The Whitsun Weddings* and in *High Windows*, and extracts from previously uncollected poems first published in the *Collected Poems*; also for extracts from *Required Writing*, *Jill* and *A Girl in Winter* by Philip Larkin.

Quotations from 'Lines on a Young Lady's Photograph Album', 'Wedding-Wind', 'Reasons for Attendance', 'Dry-Point', 'Next, Please', 'Going', 'Wants', 'Maiden Name', 'Wires', 'Church Going', 'Toads', 'Poetry of Departures', 'Tripe Time', 'Deceptions', 'I Remember, I Remember', 'Absences', 'Latest Face', 'If, My Darling', 'Skin' and 'At Grass' are reprinted from *The Less Deceived* by Philip Larkin by permission of The Marvell Press, England.

Excerpts from *High Windows*, copyright © 1974 by Philip Larkin, excerpts from *Collected Poems*, copyright © 1988, 1989 by the Estate of Philip Larkin, and excerpts from *Required Writing*, copyright © 1985 by Philip Larkin, reprinted by permission of Farrar, Straus & Giroux Inc.

Excerpts from *Jill* and *A Girl in Winter*, both copyright © 1976 by Philip Larkin, published in the United States by the Overlook Press, Lewis Hollow Road, Woodstock, NY 12498.

ABBREVIATIONS

Larkin's letters to James Ballard Sutton, now in the Brynmor Jones Library (MS DP/174/2, nos. 1–219) are referred to by date only, thus: (26.vii.50), except in the case of the few undated letters, which are referred to by number, thus: (S25). Though Larkin occasionally wrote a letter over several days the date given is always that at the head of the letter. Commonplace contractions such as '&', 'wd' and 'wch' are silently expanded.

Other abbreviations are as follows:

CP   *Collected Poems,* ed. Anthony Thwaite
            (London: The Marvell Press/Faber and
            Faber, 1988).
RW   *Required Writing: Miscellaneous pieces 1955–*
            1982 (London: Faber and Faber, 1983).
Hamilton   'Four conversations', in *London Magazine,*
            14.6 (November 1964); Ian Hamilton's
            interview with Larkin on pp. 71–7.
OBTCEV   *Oxford Book of Twentieth Century English*
            Verse (Oxford: OUP, 1973).

NOTE

Larkin's characteristic enjambements between stanzas are indicated in quotation by a double solidus, thus: 'they//Have slipped their names.'

CHRONOLOGY

1922 9 August: Philip Arthur Larkin born in Coventry, the son of Sydney Larkin, the City Treasurer, and Eva Larkin.

1930–40 Attends King Henry VIII School, Coventry.

1938 'Winter Nocturne' and 'Fragment from May' published in the school magazine, *The Coventrian*.

1940 October: Larkin goes to St John's College, Oxford.
28 November: 'Ultimatum' published in *The Listener*.

1943 June: Three poems included in *Oxford Poetry 1942–3*.
July: Awarded a first-class degree in English Language and Literature.
November: Takes up post as Librarian at Wellington in Shropshire, where he meets Ruth Bowman.

1945 *The North Ship* published by The Fortune Press.

1946 *Jill* published by The Fortune Press.
September: Takes up post as Assistant Librarian at the University College of Leicester. Monica Jones is a lecturer in the English Department.

1947   *A Girl in Winter* published by Faber and Faber.
1948   March: His father dies of cancer.
            May: Engagement to Ruth Bowman.
1948–50   Living with his mother at 12 Dixon Drive,
            Leicester.
            In The Grip of Light rejected by six publishers.
1950   Engagement to Ruth ends.
            1 October: Takes up a post as Sub-Librarian at
            Queen's University Belfast, where he meets Wini-
            fred Arnott.
1951   Distributes 100 copies of the privately printed *XX
            Poems.*
1955   21 March: Takes up post as Librarian at the
            University of Hull, where he meets Maeve
            Brennan.
            The Less Deceived published by The Marvell
            Press.
1961–71   Jazz reviewer for *The Daily Telegraph.*
1964   *The Whitsun Weddings* published by Faber and
            Faber.
1970   *All What Jazz: A record diary 1961–1968*
            published by Faber and Faber.
1970–1   Visiting Fellow at All Souls College, Oxford.
1973   *The Oxford Book of Twentieth Century English
            Verse* published by Oxford University Press.
1974   *High Windows* published by Faber and Faber.
            Moves from his flat in Pearson Park to a house in
            Newland Park, opposite the university.
1977   November: His mother dies.
1982   Monica Jones falls ill and Philip brings her to
            Hull. They live together until his death.
1983   November: *Required Writing: Miscellaneous pieces
            1955–82* published by Faber and Faber.
1984   Refuses the Laureateship after the death of John
            Betjeman.
1985   2 December: Dies of cancer at sixty-three, the
            same age as his father.
1988   *Collected Poems*, edited by Anthony Thwaite,
            published by Faber and Faber.

INTRODUCTION

I n 1973 Larkin was asked to choose two of his own poems for an anthology. He selected 'MCMXIV' and 'Send No Money', commenting:

> they might be taken as representative examples of the two kinds of poem I sometimes think I write: the beautiful and the true . . . I think a poem usually starts off either from the feeling How beautiful that is or from the feeling How true that is. One of the jobs of the poem is to make the beautiful seem true and the true beautiful, but in fact the disguise can usually be penetrated. (*Let the Poet Choose*, 102)

Beauty, a constant preoccupation of Larkin's work, takes some surprising forms, from the advertising images of 'Essential Beauty' and 'Sunny Prestatyn', through the religious yearning of the moustached women in 'Faith Healing', to 'that much-mentioned brilliance, love' in 'Love Songs in Age' and 'the strength and pain/Of being young' in 'Sad Steps'. In his 'beautiful' kind of poem, Larkin dwells longingly on images of transcendence and fulfilment, straining to assert their truth. But 'the disguise can usually be penetrated', and he poignantly fails. On a few occasions only he seems to succeed, projecting images whose beauty is impossible to 'penetrate' because they make no definable claim to 'truth': for instance the empty seascape of 'Absences', 'cleared' of the poet, the 'unfenced existence', 'out of reach' at the end of 'Here', and the 'blue air' at the end of 'High Windows', which is 'nowhere' and 'endless'. The 'true' kind of poem, on the other hand, such as 'Poetry of Departures', 'Dockery and Son' and 'Annus Mirabilis', treats the same gulf between dream and reality, but in a more explicit way, bitterly or ruefully acknowledging that all our dreams of beauty are ultimately destroyed by the blows of what happens to happen.

It is significant that Larkin chooses to describes 'MCMXIV' and 'Send No Money' in terms of beauty and truth, rather than in terms of the impact of the Great War on British society or the questionable morality of artistic detachment. When he was asked in 1957 whether writers should be 'closely concerned *in their writing* with the fundamental political and social issues of their time', he answered that 'the imagination is not the servant' of 'the intellect and the social conscience', and indeed 'may even be at variance with them' (*London Magazine*, May 1957, 38, 47). Larkin is not in any significant sense a moralist or a social satirist, and his works resist reduction to an ideological programme. The contingent social or political context of his poems should not be mistaken for their substance. He disclaimed any didactic intention in his poetry, asserting complete imaginative freedom: 'I've never been didactic, never tried to make poetry *do* things, never gone out to look for it. I waited for it to come to me, in whatever shape it chose' (*RW*, 74). He was distressed by evidence that readers were attributing programmatic commitments to his provisional embodiments of experience. 'I suppose I always try to write the truth and I wouldn't want to write a poem which suggested that I was different from what I am. In a sense that means you have to build in quite a lot of things to correct any impression of over-optimism or over-commitment' (in Hamilton, 75). Though his mention of 'over-optimism' is clearly a joke, the reference to misleading impressions of 'over-commitment' has far-reaching implications.

Despite his best efforts, Larkin proved unable to prevent readers from attributing a variety of different commitments, conscious and unconscious, to his work. He has been read, for instance, as a profoundly religious poet (Watson, 358). 'Church Going' has been interpreted as showing 'that religion offers explanations of the metaphysical elements surrounding physical life': 'The whole tone of the poem expresses doubts about the validity of atheism'

(Parkinson, 231, 224). The insistence of one American reader on finding a religious purpose in this poem, despite Larkin's emphatic denials, reduced the poet to weary sarcasm: 'Ah no, it's a great religious poem; he knows better than me – trust the tale and not the teller, and all that stuff' (in Hamilton, 73).

Other poems have been interpreted as betraying sexual-political motives. Larkin frequently expresses 'a corporate masculine perspective on sexual matters', and though he surrounds it with redeeming ironies, for some critics 'there still remains the problem of the misogyny his work expresses' (Rossen, 85). He seems, for example, to apologise for the rapist in 'Deceptions', and his attitude towards violence against women in 'Sunny Prestatyn' appears somewhat ambiguous. An 'underlying subtext' is detected, which 'seems to express resentment towards women' (Rossen, 90). It is certainly undeniable that male antagonism against women features largely in some poems, but I hope to show that Larkin's imaginative scope is broader than such a sexual-political reading allows. This 'underlying subtext' is in fact part of the artistic 'text', rather than a guilty secret.

The most widespread 'over-committed' reading of Larkin interprets much of his work as social satire, or as conscious or unconscious political ideology. Though he was quite explicit about his intentions, remarking 'I shouldn't call myself a satirist' (RW, 73), some critics nevertheless read the wry humour of his poems on advertising as moral indignation (Petch, 77; Whalen, 43), while 'Naturally the Foundation will Bear Your Expenses' is said to be a 'bitterly satirical' attack on the moral worthlessness of the persona who speaks its words (Petch, 62). A more developed version of this reading sees Larkin's poetry as the product of a profoundly conservative political ideology, marked by nostalgia for past imperial glories and despair over the decline of modern Britain (Osborne, 183; Paulin, 779–80; Whalen, 40–3). He is said to contrast 'the leisurely and poetic sense of unity in Edwardian culture' evoked in 'MCMXIV' with the modern 'decadent . . . unbeautiful commercial travesty' depicted in 'Going, Going' (Whalen, 41). Others explain his work as a complex embodiment of the political and social trends of the 1950s, during which period he came to poetic maturity. He is seen as isolated in uneasy reaction against 'the postwar social consensus' (Goodby, 132) or, more indulgently, as a spokesman for a moderate post-war Englishness: 'a poet . . . of composed and tempered English nationalism', 'the not untrue, not unkind voice of post-war England' (Heaney, 486).

Larkin's own prose comments about life and art would seem to offer support to a reading of his poems in terms of conservative or nationalist ideology. Such remarks as 'Oh, I adore Mrs Thatcher' (*RW*, 52), and 'I feel deeply humiliated at living in a country that spends more on education than defence' (in Rossen, 52) have encouraged critics to seek a political subtext even in his most delicate lyric poems. 'At Grass' and 'MCMXIV', for instance, have been read as more or less unconscious expressions of Larkin's reactionary politics (Paulin, 779). I hope that my readings will show that such political interpretations are inadequate, and that the beauty and the truth of Larkin's poems are not to be explained in terms of his 'political unconscious' (Jameson). Neither his own strident political remarks nor the social context of post-war England offers the key to his art.

Larkin's statements on aesthetics present a similarly reductive red herring. His attack on 'the aberration of modernism, that blighted all the arts' (*RW*, 216) seems to indicate a coherent, if simple aesthetic theory, as do some of his comments about his own poems: 'there's not much to *say* about my work. When you've read a poem, that's it, it's all quite clear what it means' (*RW*, 53–4). He appeals briskly to the judgement of 'the average reader' against the critics: 'There is nothing like writing poems for realizing how low the level of critical understanding is; maybe the average reader can understand what I say, but the above-average often can't' (in Hamilton, 76). All this makes Larkin into a 'middlebrow' philistine, the aesthetic counterpart of his reactionary political persona.

Commentators have not been slow to point out the contradictions in this self-projection (Motion, 17–21). Larkin intensely admired the works of many writers now generally termed 'modernist', Woolf, Mansfield and Lawrence for instance, and he was overwhelmed with confusion and pleasure when, accidentally meeting T. S. Eliot in Faber's offices, he received a vaguely encouraging remark from the older poet (*RW*, 67). Moreover a wide variety of modernist influences are detectable in his own poetry, from the imagist minimalism of 'Going' and 'Coming' to the symbolist abstraction of 'Absences', while the self-reflexiveness and 'ludic' mixture of registers in the late poem 'Sad Steps' invite the description 'postmodernist'. He has recently been termed, not altogether playfully, 'a kind of Derridian poet of absence' (Lerner, 116).

Nor had Larkin always felt the respect for the sound judgement of
the 'average reader' which he expressed in the later stages of his
career. At the time he was writing his second novel and on the
brink of his poetic maturity, he found himself, as he put it,
'handing out tripey novels to morons' (13.xii.43) in a local library in
Shropshire:

> You know, the soul-level of people is very low . . . when you
> see some bastard put down a book by Lawrence or Virginia
> Woolf as if they had just cracked a bad egg, well, it makes
> you want to kill them . . . they know nothing of the
> consuming delight of genius, or the candleflame purity of
> art the crappy-faced horseturds. (9.iii.45)

Larkin's 'anti-modernism', like his political conservatism, fails to
provide a serviceable key to his poetry. It is best seen as a strategy to
preserve his own poetic integrity, rather than as a consistent theory
of literature. Obeying his instinct not to 'go out to look for it', he
found it necessary to reject the literary fashion which, from the 1950s
onwards, canonised 'modernism' in its narrowest sense of profound
and 'difficult' obscurity. Since the only significant market for poetry
in post-war Britain was the rapidly expanding university and college
system, poets could make a living from their work only by giving
readings, or by accepting posts as 'poets in residence' employed to
explain their own poems to students. Consequently the more
difficult and 'modernist' their poetry the better. 'Writers' incomes,
as writers,' Larkin bitterly complained, 'have sunk almost below the
subsistence line. On the other hand, you *can* live by "being a writer",
or "being a poet", if you're prepared to join the cultural entertain-
ment industry, and take hand-outs from the Arts Council (not that
there are as many of them as there used to be)' (*RW*, 61-2).
Observing this phenomenon from the ambiguous position of a
salaried librarianship within the academic system, Larkin shows a
mixture of serious concern, wry amusement, and even perhaps a
touch of jealousy.

The apparent contradictions in Larkin's attitudes, and the sim-
plifications which some critics seek to impose on them, are
symptoms of the central paradox of his poetry. It is indeed very
'easy', yet at the same time it is inexhaustibly complex. There is a
real sense in which Larkin is right to say 'it's all quite clear what it

means'. But the meaning of each poem is a unique, provisional embodiment of emotions and attitudes, not a didactic statement or an ideologically motivated mystification. Larkin was as aware as any Marxist or structuralist that 'There is no unmediated experience of the world' (Belsey, 45). His work abounds in ironically 'placed' mediations, ranging from direct literary allusions (Thomas Hood, Théophile Gautier, Sidney), through dramatised self-projections (dirty old man, self-satisfied bachelor), to large cultural myths (the 'innocence' before 1914, the 'permissiveness' of the 1960s). But, ultimately, what holds these mediations of experience together is not, as some commentators have implied, conservative ideology, or stoic pessimism, or any conscious or unconscious identification with a particular historical or social group. It is something more immediate and personal, and more verbal. It is an idiomatic assurance, as of someone speaking socially to the reader. Whether in formal, pensive, angry or jocular mood, Larkin presents himself in his poems as 'a vivid and actual being who is the reverse of the "Invisible Poet" (Kenner's phrase for Eliot) invented by Modernism's quest for impersonality' (Everett 1988, 140). He is a highly 'visible' poet, who seems to have no inhibition about addressing the reader in his own candid, natural tone.

But Larkin is determined that his visibility shall not be bought at the cost of simplification or self-caricature. He is concerned not to appear 'different from what I am', which involves, as he says, finding forms of words which will preserve all the ironies of his experience, all his hesitancies, even on occasions his false pretensions. He dramatises moods and attitudes instead of trying to 'tell' the reader anything. His work makes no serious attempt to change attitudes, to challenge the reader's opinions. When you've read a Larkin poem that is indeed 'it'. To some critics this provisionalness, this absence of didactic purpose, seems to be a limitation. Larkin has been accused of narrow 'empiricism', of failing to take the ideological initiative, failing to see that life's evils can and should be 'opposed, combated, challenged' (Holderness 1989i, 113). Other readers, in contrast, feel that 'The "negativism" of Larkin's verse, the quality of the "elusive" and the "evasive" . . . may be the quality in his work that most verifies it as art'. In other words he writes 'poetry', not mere 'rhetoric' (Everett 1988, 152). He deals with a kind of truth to which moral imperatives and political prescriptions are irrelevant.

Larkin referred to his novels as episodes in his own 'soul-history'

(20.ix.45), and said that his poetry was 'nothing if not personal' (Jean Hartley, 62). As is the case with Yeats and Eliot his work must inevitably be read, on one level at least, as imaginative autobiography. In what follows I have endeavoured to deploy the facts of Larkin's life to elucidate his art rather than vice versa, avoiding 'biographism', by which the works are forced into the secondary role of illustrating or 'interpreting' the poet's life (Tallis, 76–7). It is now possible, as it has not been before, to follow Larkin's personal and artistic development through all its phases. Since his death in December 1985 the shape of his writing career, and its relationship to the events of his life, have both grown steadily clearer. The publication in October 1988 of the *Collected Poems*, edited by Anthony Thwaite, revealed for the first time when and in what order the poems were completed. This knowledge brought many new insights, since the subtle emotional sequences in which Larkin arranged his poems in the major collections published during his lifetime, *The Less Deceived* (1955), *The Whitsun Weddings* (1964) and *High Windows* (1974), often juxtapose works composed years apart at different points in his development. To see the poems rearranged in the order in which Larkin actually completed them reveals such basic facts as that the imagist poem 'Going' and the dramatic monologue 'Wedding-Wind' were both completed in 1946, over four years earlier than any of the other poems in *The Less Deceived*, and also that no fewer than eleven poems in the 1955 volume (beginning with 'At Grass', and including 'Dry-Point', 'Deceptions' and 'Absences') were completed in a sustained poetic burst in the months between January 1950 and February 1951.

Moreover, the *Collected Poems* has also added important 'new' works to the Larkin canon. Some of these poems are certainly or probably unfinished ('To My Wife', 'Long roots moor summer to our side of earth', 'The Dance'). Others may have carried too personal a charge for the poet to make them public ('An April Sunday brings the snow', 'When first we faced, and touching showed', 'Love Again'), though Larkin did not hesitate to publish other equally intimate poems during his lifetime. Larkin's will stipulated that certain of his papers, including unpublished manuscripts and diaries, should be destroyed. But, after taking legal advice, the executors destroyed only the diaries. Posterity must be grateful that the unpublished poems were thus rescued from fire or shredder. Other non-poetic material is also accumulating.

Fragments of a third and fourth novel, and also of a play, all written in the late 1940s and early 1950s, have now been deposited in the Brynmor Jones Library at the University of Hull and, though at present inaccessible, will eventually be published.

Secondary biographical material has also become increasingly available, in particular, personal documents which revise or deepen the image of the poet established during his lifetime. Larkin's diaries were shredded in accordance with the will. But much personal correspondence survives, including a sequence of over 200 often lengthy letters which the young Larkin wrote between the ages of 17 and 29 to his schoolfriend, the aspiring painter James Sutton. Of considerable literary value in their own right these letters, with their Lawrentian vitalism and expressions of aestheticist purism, serve to complicate the more familiar conservative image of Larkin conveyed by the late volume *Required Writing* (1983), in particular the interviews with the *Observer* and *Paris Review*, and the pungent introduction to *All What Jazz*.

1

'To be alive, in the flesh'

LARKIN'S LIFE

arkin's literary career falls into three phases of unequal length. The first phase, which runs from his teens until the composition of his first volume of poetry *The North Ship* (1945), and his two novels *Jill* (1946) and *A Girl in Winter* (1947), shows him full of confident vigour, determined to be a serious writer, and developing purposefully towards that goal. The second, brief but crucial and formative, phase begins with Larkin's move to Leicester University Library in 1946 and lasts until he became an Assistant Librarian at Queen's University, Belfast, in 1950. This period was one of increasing personal disappointment and frustration. His father died in 1948, and he lived for the next two years with his mother, who was frequently ill. At the same time he was suffering the emotional anxieties of a problematic engagement. His failure to marry was paralleled on the literary level by his failure to complete his third novel. He also experienced unexpected difficulty in gaining publication for his next collection of poems, finally being reduced to publishing *XX Poems* (1951) at his own expense. Nevertheless it was during this phase that he reluctantly shifted his attention from fiction to poetry and wrote his first mature poems. The third and longest phase lasts until he ceased to write serious poetry in the late 1970s. In Belfast his confidence was re-established, and in Hull, where he moved in 1955, and where he lived until his death, he found enduring stability. It was during this last phase of his career that his three major collections appeared: *The Less Deceived* (1955),

The Whitsun Weddings (1964) and *High Windows* (1974).

Philip Larkin was born in Coventry on 9 August 1922. By his own account his early life, at home and at King Henry VIII School, was uneventful:

> My father was a local government official and we lived in quite respectable houses and had a succession of maids and that sort of thing, as one did before the war. It was all very normal: I had friends whom I played football and cricket with and Hornby trains and so forth. (*RW*, 47)

This description of what 'one' considered 'all very normal' before the war establishes the bourgeois parameters which in later life Larkin made an aggressive point of not rejecting. His was no childhood of hardship and underprivilege, and his idea of the 'normal' is almost aggressively class-limited. But as the tone of this passage shows, the young Philip did not find this 'normality' stimulating or fulfilling. There is bitterness in his aphoristic characterisation of his early years as 'a forgotten boredom' in 'Coming' (*CP*, 33), and in the ironic account of his 'unspent' childhood in 'I Remember, I Remember' (*CP*, 81). Even the apparent concession in the conclusion of this poem that it was 'not the place's fault . . .//Nothing, like something, happens anywhere' (*CP*, 82) has the effect of another resentful turn of the knife. Larkin bore a profound grudge against his origins.

Larkin's father, who held the position of City Treasurer, was a man of strong views, who dominated Larkin's meek and self-effacing mother. His love of literature exercised a profound early influence on his son. However, in the realm of ideas his influence was more problematic. A devotee of D. H. Lawrence's right-wing political theories, he was deeply impressed by the achievements of fascism. Twice in the late 1930s he took his son and daughter with him to Hitler's Germany, on visits concerned with 'the study of office matters and so forth', as the poet vaguely put it in the BBC *Monitor* television programme of 1964. Larkin said little about these visits in later life, but it is easy to read between the lines: 'he took us there twice; I think this sowed the seed of my hatred of abroad – not being able to talk to anyone, or read anything' (*RW*, 47). The very blankness of the phrasing seems to indicate some concealed trauma. Clearly he was not wholly comfortable with his father's enthusiasms, and felt lost and alienated in Germany, cut off from the English language and his English books. Nevertheless the impact of his father's ideas was deep, if diffuse and complicated. The earliest letters to Sutton contain a couple of mildly disparaging references to Jews and a hint of admiration for Hitler. But by the time he is approaching twenty the young poet is full of earnest doubts: 'I think Fascism is a bad thing – I *think* it is' (S25). He concedes that 'the German system is, from all accounts, much more evil than last time' (1.iv.42). However the references to politics quickly fall off, and the later letters to Sutton, even those written at the time of Hiroshima and the momentous conference of the victorious allies at Yalta, contain only the most casual comments on international affairs:

> There is a lot in the paper today about what Russia, America, Russia, England, Russia, America and Russia are going to do with Germany after the war, but I haven't bothered to read it. I am solely concerned with the paradox of producing a fresh, spontaneous-seeming narrative out of painful rewrites and corrections.
>
> It's time I had some new clothes. These smell like a mice-cage. (9.ii.45)

It seems that the young Philip, lacking as he conceded himself, a 'conceptual or ratiocinative' mind (*RW*, 60), was unable to assert any political views of his own against those of his father. His solution was to renounce the topic altogether, which, generally speaking, is what he does in his novels and poetry. Elsewhere however his father's ideas sometimes reassert themselves powerfully, for instance in the reactionary comments of his later prose writings and interviews.

In one of the earliest letters to Sutton (begun three days after war was declared) Larkin dramatises his ironic detachment from his family life by means of a caricature sketch entitled 'Portrait of the Author and Family, 1939'. It is a remarkably assured piece of satire to have been produced by a seventeen-year-old youth. In cartoon manner, balloons emerge from the characters' mouths. 'Pop', sitting back in his chair, gesticulating and holding a newspaper bearing the headline 'WAR', gives vent to a mixture of fascist propaganda and Lawrentian apocalyptics:

> The british government have started this war . . . Hitler has done all he could for peace . . . well, all I hope is that we get

11

smashed to Hades . . . our army is useless. A. R. P.? Ha, ha!
This is the end of civilisation . . . after all, man has to be
superseded sooner or later . . . we're only a stage in the
earth's development . . . a very unimportant stage, too . . .
(6.ix.39)

'Mop' (Larkin's mother) sits opposite knitting, wondering 'what we
ought to have for lunch tomorrow', ticking off her son for scraping
his shoes on the floor and moderately hoping that 'Hitler falls on a
banana skin'. Her daughter stands at one edge of the picture, talking
monotonously about the trivia of her social life. Philip sits at the
other edge, pen in hand, blushing, with a huge exclamation-mark
over his head, a doleful picture of adolescent alienation.

A school-friend of the time has given his impression of the
constrained and correct atmosphere of the household in which
Larkin grew up: '. . . in spite of the unfailing graciousness of Mrs
Larkin's welcome, the atmosphere of Philip's home, with its
intimidating tidiness, its highly waxed furniture and the practice of
hushed conversation, impressed me as solemn' (Hughes 1982, 21).
As a schoolboy Philip appeared to be in awe of his father, about
whom he never spoke. He dressed 'soberly', but 'not without
elegance, or even panache', preferring bow ties (like his father), and
acting older than his years (20). At school he showed 'a profound
distaste for all forms of physical activity' (17). But despite this, and
the fact that he took 'some sort of prize' in all his later years in
school, he succeeded in avoiding victimisation or hostility: 'In
general, he was well-liked and quite without enemies: popular with
the boys because he mocked the staff, and with the staff because he
was invariably polite towards them' (19). He was already involved in
literary activity, and though he had adopted his father's 'total
disbelief in Christianity', this did not prevent him from composing
'blank verse choruses for a passion play for Holy Week 1939'
(Hughes 1982, 21, 18). His first published poems appeared in the
school magazine, *The Coventrian*, in late 1938 and in 1939 (*CP*, 225–
7, 230), lyrically descriptive pieces with titles like 'Winter Nocturne',
'Fragment from May' and 'Street Lamps'. Their style slips between
Keatsian mellifluousness, a formal artifice reminiscent of Gray, and
extravagant conceits in imitation of early Eliot.

At the time war broke out Larkin was preparing to go to Oxford
University to read English. He later laid right-wing emphasis on the

fact that he was not a 'scholarship' boy: '. . . thanks to my father's generosity, my education was at no time a charge on public or other funds'. It is perhaps important to the later development of the poet that he escaped the general fate of his generation during the war. Most of his fellow students at Oxford were soon called up. Larkin's eyesight, however, was too poor for him to be accepted into the army, and he spent the full three years as an undergraduate in Oxford between 1940 and 1943. During this time his friends Kingsley Amis, James Sutton and others disappeared at intervals to serve in the forces. It was a strange period of subdued austerity for the university, a strangeness reflected in Larkin's first novel *Jill* (1946), which he wrote in the months following his graduation. Many of the letters of the time, however, express a contented enjoyment of life, and reveal that, despite the war, he lived out as fully as he could the life of an Oxford aesthete. In the 1963 Introduction to *Jill* he insists with hindsight that his was not 'the Oxford of Michael Fane and his fine bindings, or Charles Ryder and his plovers' eggs' (*RW*, 18). But the letters show that, as a student, he had evolved his own version of Oxford preciosity and dandyism. He dwells rapturously on the fine detail of American jazz recordings, sports a new bow tie with pride, and enjoys the astonishment of the lower-class passers-by as he parades through Oxford, unshaven and with a cigarette dangling from his lips, in a pair of new red trousers – an episode accompanied by one of his most vivid little pen-sketches: 'Coo!'; 'Ere, look at im'; 'Look at the pansy with the pink pants!' (16.ix.41).

The mannered romantic poems which he was writing at this time, many of them later collected in *The North Ship* (1945), are the poetic reflection of this youthful lifestyle, an accomplished mix of Yeats and Auden – and later of Dylan Thomas, whose hilarious imitations of other poets reading their own verse, delivered at the University Poetry Society, Larkin long remembered. But his letters brim with a quite indiscriminate *joie de vivre*, which overflows as readily into ebullient obscenity as into the extravagant aesthetic poses of his 'serious' poetry. A letter written during the Christmas vacation of his second year at Oxford suddenly breaks off with the remark: 'I have just farted with the sound of an iron ruler twanging in a desk-lid and the smell of a west wind over a decaying patch of red cabbages' (31.xii.41). Earlier in the same month he had composed a wicked parody of Keats's 'La Belle Dame Sans Merci':

And this is why I shag alone
Ere half my creeping days are done[.]
The wind coughs sharply in the stone,
    There is no sun

To light my way to bed: the leaves
Are brown upon the icy tree;
The swallows all have left the eaves
    Silently, silently.

He continues: 'This is the latest work of the brilliant new Post-Masturbationist Poet, Shaggerybox McPhallus. His new book of verse, "The Escaped Cock", deals almost exclusively with problems of intense spiritual value, which are yet so universal in their application as to be ensured of a wide public' (4.xii.41).

Philip also relished the more commonplace mischiefs of male undergraduate life. Early in 1942 he wrote to Sutton 'Things are all right – except that a horrible tough is trying to find me to beat me up because I helped wreck his room' (7.iii.42). This episode perhaps was the biographical basis for the scene in *Jill* in which Kemp vandalises the room of Whitbread, the contemptible, hard-working scholarship boy. Later he summed up his state of mind as his precious days as a student drew to an end: 'You ask me what I am doing – I am preparing to take Finals, and the prospect is an expanding shite. I am also dressed in red trousers, shirt, and white pullover, and look very beautiful . . . In fact I am happy' (14.v.43). Though affecting idleness and ignorance, Larkin had not neglected his academic work and in due course achieved a first-class degree. His response to the news is a little masterpiece of elated excitement:

My dear Jim – in whatever state this reaches you, at peace or at war (for I hear the 8th Army is engaged in Sicily), asleep or awake, in sorrow or in joy, I simply must dance my little dance and tell you that I have got a FIRST in my schools!! Oh, how clever I am! Oh, how infinite and wise in my faculties! A star descends onto my forehead! It is all the more remarkable because I made numerous blunders and knew sweet bugger all about my subject. That means I was so clever and penetrating and witty that my superior mind shone incandescently above all the ather – ather – ather wurr – wurr – maroook!! (surprised belch.)

I hope all this doesn't sound too big-'eaded, as Montgomery would say. But a first is a very exciting thing. Aldous Huxley got one. (18.vii.43)

His comic imitation of his own stammer and his self-ironic jubilation are disarmingly ridiculous.

In the early 1940s Larkin's ideas about art separate themselves antithetically into an aestheticist devotion to 'beauty', and Freudian scepticism. The eighteen-year-old undergraduate paints himself as an extravagant aesthete: 'Once more on the lawns in brilliant sun. Ah, beauty, beauty! What is Truth? Balls. What is Love? Shite. What is God? Bugger. Ah, but what is beauty? Boy, you got sump'n there. I should like to know' (23.vi.41). Three years later he argues that 'art is as near religion as one can get' (5.vii.44), and two years later again he hotly defends Walter Pater's famous phrase: 'Do you hear any disparaging talk about "Art for Art's sake"? It annoys me. For what other sake can art possibly be undertaken? Let them tell me that' (16.x.46). However, alongside these confident assertions of artistic faith occur less elevated speculations: 'Did Freud say the sexual instinct was at the bottom of everything? Anyway, I'm sure art is a form of sexual perversion' (16.xii.40). This reflection clearly worried him, and made him unwilling to explore further for fear of what he might find. 'As for the vision itself, it's got something to do with sex. I don't know what, and I don't particularly want to know. It's not surprising because obviously two creative forces will be in alliance' (28.xii.40). In 1942–3 he wrote down ninety-five of his dreams in an attempt at Freudian self-analysis, stopping early in 1943: 'I have dropped my dream-business (where? into the Thames?): presumably I am the Individuated man' (7.i.43). Nevertheless, a few months later, he was still toying with the idea that his art was a morbid substitute for life:

> Art is awfully *wrong*, you know. Art is born of, and should generate, delight in life. But the delight it generates is purely *vicarious* – i.e. it's fake. Appreciating the beauty of life from a book is as bad as getting a horn from a dirty picture (not a G. H. Horne – cubes, cubes.) Or don't you agree? Let me know what you think. (12.vii.43)

15

Characteristically Larkin left this debate unresolved, preferring to write poetry rather than dissect his poetic creativity. It still echoes through his later work, however, in the psychological motifs and terminology of such poems as 'This Be The Verse' (*CP*, 180) and 'Love Again' (*CP*, 215), and also in 'Jake Balokowsy's' reference to the poet in 'Posterity' as 'One of those old-type *natural* fouled-up guys' (*CP*, 170).

Larkin seems genuinely to have felt no guilt at missing any first-hand experience of the war. In *Jill* the Coventry Blitz of November 1940 is fictionally depicted as a traumatic rite of passage for the maturing protagonist, rather than as an act of German aggression which he has a duty to resist (see also Hughes 1989). Larkin's letters to Sutton show an undisguised apprehension at the prospect of having to serve in the army, and to suffer the interruption of his artistic development: 'We have all the hell of a way to go, both as artists and as human beings. And I somehow don't think the Army will help, except in the purely negative way of steering you clear of a war complex. Fuck and bugger the war' (10.xi.41). Despite this reference, he shows no sign of a 'war complex' himself, apart perhaps from a defensive irritability in speaking about it. In contrast, his fear of the brutalising influence of army life is expressed bluntly and without embarrassment:

> Perhaps you think I am being a bit selfish but I just don't want to go into the Army. I want to pretend it isn't there: that there's no war on. When I do get into it, it will be a hell of a struggle of readjustment. I dare say I shall get over it in about 3 months. But they'll be a dose of Hell.
> I wonder if suicide is *very* easy? (20.xi.41)

A short time later, after he had obtained his exemption, his expressions of relief are equally unembarrassed, and he seems determined to cling to his own aesthetic enjoyments in spite of everything:

> Roars of a bestial nature from outside indicate that some of the British Army is in the vicinity. Poor bastards. I never cease thanking my stars that I have been spared – I hope – at

least the grosser outrages of the barrack square. I fuck the
Army. Shag them all.

Jazz is a *good thing*. (22.i.42)

One might speculate whether Larkin's attitude would have changed
had any of his close friends or relatives been killed. But as it is, it
seems that he was able to view the war in the light of a general
catastrophe, the worst hardships of which, by lucky accident, he was
spared, allowing him to continue the important work of perfecting
his art. The letters show no interest in the specific conduct or politics
of the war, or in its atrocities. The occasional mentions of large
historical events always come second to his jazz enthusiasms, his
reflections on art, and his despondencies about his own writing.

Larkin's priorities are clearly seen in a letter written on VE day, 8
May 1945, as he moped about with mild food-poisoning, and
listened to the radio: 'I listened to Churchill blathering out of turn
this afternoon, and the King this evening. But all day I have had a
headache and felt despondent. The second draft of the novel has
reached p. 22.' This new novel, originally entitled *The Kingdom of
Winter*, and eventually published as *A Girl in Winter* in 1947,
eschews specific reference to public themes. Though the protagonist
is a foreign refugee in England we discover nothing about the
circumstances of her exile, the fate of her family, or even her
nationality. It is scarcely surprising that Larkin shunned the
'tomfoolery' of the crucial 1945 election, and failed to vote. 'What
have I to do with it?' he exclaimed impatiently (11.vii.45). In a later
letter he finds himself straying momentarily into a judgement on
'these dogfaced sods of Soviets: ugly soulless buggers they sound',
and at once draws back, with oddly vehement self-dismissal: 'Still, I
don't know anything at all about anything, and it[']s no use
pretending I do' (10.iii.46).

On coming down from Oxford in 1943 Larkin had had no clear
idea what he wanted to do, except of course to be a writer (at this
time he still intended to write novels). At length the authorities
intervened, as he drolly recollected in 1979:

> I tried twice to get into the Civil Service but the Civil
> Service didn't want me, and I was sitting at home quietly
> writing *Jill* when the Ministry of Labour wrote to me
> asking, very courteously, what I was doing exactly. This

17

scared me and I picked up the *Birmingham Post* and saw that
an urban district council in Shropshire wanted a Librarian,
so I applied and got it. (*RW*, 51)

In retrospect Larkin saw this as an 'inspired choice' of career:
'Librarianship suits me – I love the feel of libraries – and it has just
the right blend of academic interest and administration that seems to
match my particular talents, such as they are' (*RW*, 51). At the time,
however, the feelings he confided to Sutton were distinctly
ambiguous. On the one hand, he possessed a stinging contempt for
the middle-class, middlebrow reading public whom it would be his
task to serve in Wellington: 'I know sweet fuck-all about librarianship. ("Ah yes? You want *The Mortal Storm*, by Phyllis Arse, do
you? Er – pardon me – I mean *Bottome*, yers, yers, of course . . .
Well, do you? You do? Then permit me to inform you that you are
the son of a whore . . .")' (29.x.43). And once he had taken up his
post he lamented his lot with delicate fastidiousness: 'I feel it is not
at all a suitable occupation for a man of acute sensibility and genius'
(13.xii.43). On the other hand he did enjoy the freedom of being
entirely his own master, the library having no other staff at the time.
He quickly devised a characteristically Larkinesque strategy that
would preserve his artistic freedom while not getting him into
trouble: 'I intend to devote myself to writing and doing my boring
job without enthusiasm or slackness. I only took it on account of
being able to write in the intervals: it's not so easy, I must say, but
it[']s possible' (22.iii.44). Less than three years later Larkin had
made sufficient progress with his 'boring job' to secure a post as an
Assistant Librarian at what was then Leicester University College,
and in September 1946 left this Shropshire backwater behind him.

During his years in Leicester between 1946 and 1950 the smooth
career of untroubled artistic creativity which Larkin had mapped out
for himself faltered and seemed in danger of coming to nothing. The
most serious threat to his composure was an emotional entanglement
with Ruth Bowman, whom he first met when she was a schoolgirl in
Wellington, and who subsequently moved to London to train as a
teacher. At first Larkin was very reticent about this relationship, but
it is clear enough that he felt threatened by it, not only personally,
but also artistically:

What worries me at the moment is this girl I believe I

mentioned in my last letter. It is rather a disturbing experience to have someone utterly dependent on you, it puts one's least thoughts and actions under a microscope (at any rate, to oneself) and short-circuits one's processes. One has no elbow-room. I feel as if my wings were in danger of being clipped. And it worries me also to find that I am a long way off being capable of any emotion as simple as what is called love. It seems limiting and insulating to me. (31.x.45)

'Wedding-Wind' (*CP*, 11), written in September 1946, seems to represent an imaginative attempt by the poet to break out of such selfish limitations by empathising with a newly-married woman. There can be little doubt that Philip's disastrous engagement to Ruth was precipitated by the emotional shock of his father's death in March 1948. The poet, then 25, was deeply distressed by his father's sudden illness, and one of the most moving of his early mature works is an elegy on his father, 'An April Sunday brings the snow', completed on 4 April 1948 (*CP*, 21), but not included in any of the collections published during his lifetime.

Six weeks after writing this poem, in May 1948, he and Ruth Bowman became engaged. His announcement of the event to Sutton is made in a revealingly awkward manner:

To tell you the truth I have done something rather odd myself – got engaged to Ruth on Monday. You know I have known her since 1943 or 4; well, we have gone on seeing each other until the point seemed to arrive when we either had to start taking it seriously or else drop it. I can't say I welcome the thought of marriage, as it appears to me from the safe side of it, but nor do I want to desert the only girl I have met who doesn't instantly frighten me away. It has been putting me backwards and forwards through the hoop for a long time now: I still console myself with the thought that all is not yet lost. No one could imagine me to be madly in love, and indeed I'm more 'madly out of love' than in love, so much so that I suspect all my isolationist feelings as possibly harmful and certainly rather despicable. 'Are you a bloody valuable vase, man, to be kept so carefully?'

He continues in this unhappy vein, suggesting that the engagement is intended to help her over her final examinations, 'which she was in a fair way to buggering up', and ending with a weird comic image from the Canadian humorist Stephen Leacock: 'Occasionally Leacock's image of putting one's finger into machinery which goes on until it is halted by one's suspenders occurs to me – I don't know how it'll turn out. It's either the best thing I've done or the worst thing' (18.v.48).

After qualifying, Ruth secured a post in the Midlands to be near him, and Philip's letters to Sutton become polarised between anxious strictures on his own selfishness and the irritated insistence that he needs his freedom. It may be that a crisis occured later in 1948. At any rate there is a sudden four-month gap in the letters to Sutton (29.xi.48 – 24.iii.49), and when Larkin resumes communication it is in a very grim tone. He parallels the failure of the relationship with his difficulties in writing his third novel:

> I have given up my novel and Ruth has given up me, not seeing, as you might say, any future in it. Nor do I! Therefore I am living a disagreeable life at this remnant of a home, with a general sense of being buggered up, and a generally despicable character. I could go on for hours about myself, but I fancy I had better not. (24.iii.49)

An undertone of relief is audible here, despite his misery and self-disgust. The relationship however stumbled along from crisis to crisis, and in May 1950 Larkin was still tangled in self-analysis and egotistical petulance:

> It's all very complicated and certainly not creditable to me, who have been piddling about like a finger-chewing curate for five years. Why haven't I married her? Oh well, partly because she doesn't 'send' me, partly because she did so want me to, and made no bones about it. But . . . but . . . but . . . Well anyway. (20.v.50)

He is brutal with himself, lurching from extravagant self-disgust to withering sarcasm:

> Now my illusion of marriage is pleasant. But the reality

would be hell. Or is it the other way round? . . . BULL-SHITBAG!!!!! Christ knows what I'm going to do. I feel D. H. L. would sum it all up in a few words. '. . . meanwhile Philip gnawed his fingers, being a Willy Wetleg, and tried to decide whether A Woman was worth more to him than His Art. His most fundamental feeling was one of surprise that any woman should be prepared to marry him at all . . .' (3.vii.50)

Even at this point it seems, he might still have gone through with it, despite everything. But by the end of July 1950 the break had finally become irreversible:

I have not got engaged. Despite my fine feelings, when it really comes down to terms of furniture and loans from the bank something unmeltable and immoveable rises up in me – something infantile, cowardly, regressive. But *it won't be conquered.* I'm a romantic bastard. Remote things seem desirable. Bring them close, and I start shitting myself. (26.vii.50)

As his engagement to Ruth faltered, his relationship with Monica Jones, a lecturer in the English Department at Leicester, which had become established in 1948, deepened. Though Philip had not met Monica before he came to Leicester, they had both been to Oxford University, and moreover, their literary passions largely coincided. This was to develop into the most durable liaison of the poet's life and must soon have made any prospect of marriage to Ruth impossible, though intriguingly Philip makes absolutely no mention of Monica in any of his letters to Sutton.

Such poems as 'Deceptions' (*CP*, 32) and 'If, My Darling' (*CP*, 41), both completed in the early months of 1950, reflect the grim, guilt-ridden impasse which the engagement had become by this time. But, as these works show, Larkin did not always see his difficulties over the idea of marriage in purely personal terms. At times he depicted them as part of a larger conflict between creative freedom and domestic responsibility. His usual attitude is that 'art' and 'life' are mutually interdependent: 'Art is born of, and should generate delight in life' (12.vii.43). However, in his discussions of his relationship with Ruth this confident aesthetic language is increasingly replaced by a heavily moralised vocabulary in which 'life' and 'art' become polarised opposites:

> What mainly worries me, if you'll excuse my speaking on my own affairs for the moment, is a strengthening suspicion that in my character there is an antipathy between 'art' and 'life'. I find that once I 'give in' to another person, as I have given in not altogether voluntarily, but almost completely, to Ruth, there is a slackening and dulling of the peculiar artistic fibres that makes it impossible to achieve that mental 'clenching' that crystallises a pattern and keeps it still while you draw it . . . I find, myself, that this letting-in of a second person spells death to perception and the desire to express, as well as the ability.

He adds with humility that if his talent needs this kind of protection then it must be a modest one: 'It's not much of a talent that can be overthrown by deeper contact with other people' (7.iv.46). It might be felt that Larkin is here simply rationalising the fact that he did not happen to be in love. As we have seen, Ruth did not 'send' him. However that may be, by 1950 he certainly felt that in rejecting marriage he was not only freeing himself from a personal entanglement, but, more importantly, protecting his art. The idea that marriage would destroy the imaginative freedom of the artist recurs in several poems of the early 1950s, such as 'To My Wife' (*CP*, 54) and 'Reasons for Attendance' (*CP*, 80).

The turn of the decade was a period of acute frustration for Larkin. Not only was he embroiled in his engagement, he was also, in his late twenties, living with his mother. Shortly after his father's death he had arranged the sale of the family home in Warwick (where the family had moved some time before) and bought 12 Dixon Drive, Leicester, where they lived for the next two years. He became acutely depressed, but was unable to break free. His home background, which had always seemed constricting to his spirit, now seemed inescapable, and his long-standing dislike of it became concentrated. A letter of April 1949 contains a characteristic complaint:

> Home appears bloody sodding hell, as usual. God! When will the tiny light appear, the end of this perpetual tunnel?

> Must one wait for everyone to die off before breathing and
> relaxing?. . . Tomorrow a jolly excursion to my father's
> grave, plus a pair of bastard silly old relatives, the whole
> well soused with irritation and complaining. (19.iv.49)

The unsatisfactoriness of his relations with all his family was
constantly present to him. As he summed it up later in life in an
interview: 'I wouldn't want it thought that I didn't like my parents.
I did like them. But at the same time they were rather awkward
people and not very good at being happy. And these things rub off'
(*RW*, 48).

Larkin's feelings about his mother remain throughout her life a
mixture of absolute intimacy and helpless dissatisfaction. In April
1951 he speculates in a letter on the degree to which he will ever
succeed in disengaging himself imaginatively from her psychological
legacy: '. . . unwanted detachment, inexplicable lassitudes (sluggish-
ness) and lack of feeling about anything in particular'. He draws a
quaint little sketch of himself, arms thrown out, shouting euphori-
cally 'I'm free! I'm free!', while in fact he is buried up to the waist in
the ground with an ominous octopus-like tangle of roots firmly
wound round one ankle (24.iv.51). 'Mother, Summer, I' depicts
mother and son united by their repressions. Just as she fears the
thunderstorms of summer, preferring the continuous rain and brittle
frost of autumn, so the poet ('I her son') finds himself unable to
'confront' the perfect happiness of summer days, and awaits 'A time
less bold, less rich, less clear:/ An autumn more appropriate' (*CP*,
68). 'Reference Back' similarly unites mother and son in intimate
failure, as the record of Oliver's *Riverside Blues* forms a momentary
bridge 'From your unsatisfactory age/To my unsatisfactory prime'
(*CP*, 106). The sense of masculine guilt which colours the poet's
relationships with women must derive to some extent from this
feeling for his mother, and perhaps also from his reaction to his
father's treatment of her. He continued to write regularly to her
throughout her life, twice a week until 1970, and thereafter a line or
two every day until her death in 1977 at the age of 91. Shortly after
her death he added the last two stanzas to 'Aubade' (*CP*, 208–9), one
of his last and bleakest major poems (George Hartley 1988, 4).

But an equally intense source of anxiety for Larkin during the late
1940s was the problem of his literary career. He found it impossible
to write a third novel, though he continued to work at the task for

five years. At the same time he experienced difficulties in getting his poetry into print. His second collection, *In the Grip of Light*, was rejected by six publishers and eventually he was reduced to producing a booklet, *XX Poems*, at his own expense, and sending copies to poets and editors. But by the time *XX Poems* was published in 1951 he had already created his own light at the end of the tunnel by securing the post of Sub-Librarian at Queen's University, Belfast, where he went to live in October 1950. This move to Ireland cut several knots at one stroke. He threw off the entanglements of his origins, made the break with Ruth Bowman and put himself beyond the immediate demands of his mother. At last he found himself able to live and write as he wished. During his first months in Belfast he continued to explore the bitter aftermath of his engagement in poems such as 'No Road' (*CP*, 47), 'To My Wife' (*CP*, 54), and 'Marriages' (*CP*, 63). But he also struck new, less anxious notes. In the month following his arrival in Belfast he wrote 'Absences' (*CP*, 49), and two or three months later, in February 1951, 'Latest Face' (*CP*, 53).

Sutton's first and only visit to Belfast was not a success. The poet, it seems, was too absorbed in his new life to pay enough attention to his old schoolmate, who took offence at his casualness. The Sutton letters thus come to an abrupt end in January 1952. However, the few letters written to Sutton during this first year in Belfast already show a new assurance and contentment in Larkin's tone. There is a tangible release of tension, a sense of untrammelled freedom. The letters swing between elusive poetic symbol ('By the Gor the weather is fine these days – life turns and beckons to me like an underwater swimmer in a soundless tank, beguiling, impossible' (14.x.51)) and a sense of crude physical well-being:

> I should think, next to good health, an independent income is the best thing a man could have. I adore not working. Every Sunday I wallow in the luxury of freedom, lying ['in' deleted] on my bed in sheer exultant laziness: to do that every day. Golly! One would feel like a great steaming manure heap in the sun, lazy, pregnant, valuable. (21.i.52)

Later Larkin saw the move to Belfast as a crucial turning-point in his life: 'After finishing my first books, say by 1945, I thought I had come to an end. I couldn't write another novel, I published nothing.

My personal life was rather harassing. Then in 1950 I went to Belfast, and things reawoke somehow' (*RW*, 68). He also remarked that the physical conditions of his solitary life in a top-floor flat in Belfast were particularly favourable for writing poetry: 'The best writing conditions I ever had were in Belfast, when I was working at the University there. Another top-floor flat, by the way. I wrote between eight and ten in the evenings, then went to the University bar till eleven, then played cards or talked with friends till one or two' (*RW*, 58). The masculine insouciance of this lifestyle seems to have come as a relief after the feminine complications of the previous two years. Later, in 1970, Larkin gave a nostalgic and highly symbolic poetic expression to this crude male solidarity in his celebration of the 'secret bestial piece' of 'The Card-Players' (*CP*, 177).

Monica Jones paid visits to Belfast, though his relationship with her did not prevent him developing new attachments, one of which, to Winifred Arnott, a trainee in the University Library, though ephemeral in biographical terms, gave him the occasion for two of his most beautiful poems: the first, 'Lines on a Young Lady's Photograph Album' (*CP*, 71), completed late in 1953, and the second, 'Maiden Name' (*CP*, 101), early in 1955. As the poems show, this vivacious young woman elicited from the poet a delicate, even protective, affection, quite different in quality from anything he felt for the other women in his life. Shortly after they met she travelled to London to complete her training, and there she became engaged to be married. When she returned to Ireland, however, she and Philip began to see a great deal of each other, as before. The fiancé, hearing of this, wrote Larkin a letter of complaint, and the poet, having no intention of entering upon marriage himself, withdrew. 'Long roots moor summer to our side of earth' (*CP*, 96) expresses Philip's feelings on the day she married, 12 June 1954, and a distinct wistfulness also underlies 'Maiden Name', written some six months later.

It was while he was at Belfast that Larkin entered upon the most sustained period of productivity of his career, preparing his first major collection of poetry, eventually published as *The Less Deceived*. The Dolmen Press expressed an interest in the volume, but fell victim to financial problems, and Larkin found a publisher in the small Marvell Press, recently founded by George and Jean Hartley in Hull. By this time Larkin was seeking to return to the mainland of

England, and by a strange coincidence he secured the post of Librarian at the University of Hull, arriving in March 1955. The Hartleys brought out the book six months later. In Hull his emotions stabilised, and his life settled into a pattern which changed little for the next three decades. The anchor of his personal life during these years was Monica Jones, with whom he developed a relationship totally different from that with either Ruth Bowman or Winifred Arnott. A flamboyant, self-assured and articulate woman, she offered Philip intellectual as well as emotional companionship, though what role she played in Larkin's development as a poet is difficult to assess. Though he lived and worked in an academic environment throughout his life, he always expressed horror at the literary analysis or 'teaching' of poetry, any involvement in which on his own part he felt would have destroyed his creativity. Nevertheless, through Monica Jones he was constantly exposed to the eclecticism and flexibility of a teacher involved with the full historical range of literature. It may be suspected that this relationship contributed something to the free mix of styles which makes itself apparent in Larkin's most mature poetry.

One of Monica Jones's students at Leicester in the late 1960s well remembers the dramatic quality of her lectures, which she would deliver in the miniskirt and fishnet tights fashionable at that period. The extensive marginal notes she made on this student's essay on Yeats, written in 1968, show the combative and stimulating nature of her teaching style, and demonstrate the passionate devotion to poetry which drew her and Larkin together. With refreshing scepticism she calls Yeats an 'old *poseur* and exaggerater', and her reading of 'The Lake Isle of Innisfree' is wilfully prosaic, in a way which Larkin would have greatly appreciated:

> I always think the 9 bean rows bit is nonsense – 9 bean rows, and *live alone*; anybody who's ever tried to keep up with even one or two bean rows in August will know that this is rubbish; better *one* bean row and 9 hives for the honey bee – honey will *keep*. This is a bit frivolous, perhaps, but not altogether so. Anyway, it's something to think abt; shd this *sort* of poem tell the practical truth? 9 bean rows! The liar! It's all artificial and this proves that it is – this is me at my most militant.

She shows a preference for the ballad conventions of 'Down by the

Salley Gardens' over the elaborate mythologies of Yeats's later
verse: 'The *Salley Gardens* I think does go deeper than a lot that Y.
says. Who cares abt the bloody gyres? Everybody cares abt love.' At
the end of the essay she discusses at length the relative merits of
Yeats and Hardy, coming to conclusions of which Larkin would
certainly have approved, then launches into a candid argument with
herself about the possible limitations of her responses:

> In the meantime, have you read Hardy's poetry? It seems to
> me that at present it is rather difficult to appreciate Yeats
> and Hardy as it requires some catholicity to appreciate,
> *truly*, both Donne & Milton. 'As of today', as the Americans
> say, I am so strongly for Hardy that I'm probably incapable
> of seeing Yeats properly. I shan't change. But of course I
> can see a lot in Yeats to admire; he could *write* – no doubt
> abt that, tho' his imagery is somewhat limited & there's
> altogether too much of the Mask & the parade . . . Some-
> times I'm persuaded (I don't mean by other people) that
> he's good; sometimes he seems just like a mad tinkle on the
> very edge of life.

Monica Jones seems to have played the invaluable role of sympathetic first reader, discussing Larkin's poems with him and even
occasionally assisting in their composition. The odd medieval word
'losels' in 'Toads Revisited', for instance, was included at her
suggestion.

As time went by a pattern developed in their relationship. Monica
and Philip would meet every three or four weeks, in Leicester or
Hull, and would go on holiday together each year, sometimes to Sark
in the Channel Islands. John Osborne, a lecturer at Hull University,
who lived for a short time in the flat below Larkin's in the early
1970s, has related the impact of one of Monica Jones's eruptions into
the usual silence of his neighbour's life:

> The first time I met her she was swaying drunkenly in the
> front doorway of the house, a buxom woman in a tight
> pullover and toreador pants . . . Throughout that weekend
> the Jazz was almost continuous, shouts and laughter were
> frequent, the communal dustbins were more than usually
> full of empty alcohol bottles, and riotous noises replaced the

deathly silence usually emanating from the flat above.

(Osborne, 183)

Their relationship was not without its tensions, however. She remained in Leicester while, as a friend of the time remarks, Philip 'was never short of women who wanted to marry him' in Hull. He was not 'faithful' in any conventional way. The long unfinished poem 'The Dance' (CP, 154–8), on which he worked between June 1963 and May 1964, shows him embarking on a new romance with all the tongue-tied embarrassment of youth. His relationship with the woman referred to in this poem, Maeve Brennan, a colleague in the University Library, had become established in 1961 when he was 38, and it is Maeve's hands which are heard clapping at the end of the exquisite 'Broadcast', written in this year (CP, 140). From the beginning, however, their relationship was complicated by reservations on both sides. Broken off after a quarrel in 1973, it resumed again in the following year, and finally moderated to friendship in 1978. In 1975 Philip had become involved with another woman, to whom he addressed the love poem 'When first we faced, and touching showed' (CP, 205), and 'Morning at last: there in the snow' (CP, 206). The brutal and despairing 'Love Again' (CP, 215), completed in 1979 but begun some years earlier, also concerns this other woman.

There is ample evidence that Larkin was an attractive man, but his sense of the difficulty and disappointments of his various relationships caused him to project himself as a comically pathetic failure. His jokes about his ugliness, together with his declarations of envy for the more glamorous and successful Kingsley Amis, were a means of coping with this unresolved complication in his life by fictionalising and ironising it. Another more commonplace means of preserving his sexual equilibrium was pornographic fantasy. Pornography provided him with a certain measure of vicarious imaginative control over the 'irritant' (CP, 36) of sexual desire, and perhaps also offered an escape from the problematic demands of real women. Though it may indicate a certain fear of women and a desire to humiliate them, pornography in Larkin's case seems also to have been a method of preserving himself (and his women friends) from the disastrous intensities of relationships like that with Ruth. The Sutton letters show that the undergraduate Larkin had written pornographic prose fantasies featuring his female acquaintances, and it seems certain that pornography was one of the elements in the later journals which he directed to be destroyed after his death. He kept a pair of opera glasses by his office window overlooking the main University concourse, in order to watch the women students passing by in their miniskirts. With the help of one of his literary friends he amassed a large collection of pornographic books and magazines. A female friend in Hull relates how, innocent of such things, she expressed inquisitiveness about this strange male preoccupation. He responded by opening a large cupboard full of both literary and photographic pornography, and selected what she assumes must have been a comparatively mild sample: 'photographs of grown-up women in gymslips', and a story featuring wife-swapping and spanking. When she asked him what it was *for*, he replied (somewhat embarrassed) 'to wank to, or with, or at'.

After an initial eighteen months of discomfort in various digs in Hull Larkin had moved into a University flat on the top floor of a Victorian house overlooking the greenery and wide spaces of Pearson Park. It was not until 1964, almost a decade after his arrival, that he bought his first car, and until then he would cycle to the city centre shops after work each Saturday, and then go on, with his provisions in a knapsack, to Hessle just outside Hull, where George and Jean Hartley lived (Jean Hartley, 72). Once a month he would visit his mother, and on the intervening Sundays he would go on walking or cycling expeditions 'all over what was then the East Riding', or would wander round the wilderness of Spring Bank Cemetery, near to his flat (Brennan 28-9). At the time of his arrival the library staff consisted of only two men and nine women, almost all of them about twenty years old, and Maeve Brennan remembers these early years as a 'happy, carefree era' full of 'innocent charm and fun': 'The highlight for us was tea at his place where he invariably provided toasted crumpets spread with Gentleman's Relish, and Earl Grey tea, served in his primrose-decorated china tea service which was brought out specially on these occasions' (30). With the Hartleys he showed his more earthy side, concocting 'shockingly ribald parodies of great poets', and frequently indulging in 'a good moan about the aridity of his sex life', fantasising enviously about the adventures of his academic colleagues among the women students (Jean Hartley, 78, 95).

Meanwhile his 'boring job' grew immensely in its scope, and he rose conscientiously to the challenge. At the time he took up his post in Hull in 1955, the institution was embarking on a major expansion. Until the previous year, indeed, it had still been a mere University College. He at once became involved with ambitious plans for a new library building, to which he devoted much time and thought, suggesting important modifications. This was completed in 1959. But already by 1963 a new, larger extension was in hand, which was eventually completed in 1970. At one point during the 1970s staff numbers in the new library rose to over a hundred, though at the time Larkin died this had been reduced to eighty. Kingsley Amis relates how he overheard two lecturers in the Engineering Department at Swansea praising the achievement of the librarian at Hull, clearly without any knowledge that he was also a poet (1991, 59). In the wider field of librarianship Larkin promoted the cause of the collection and preservation of modern literary manuscripts, presenting a paper on this topic in 1979 at the Standing Conference of National and University Libraries in King's College, London (*RW*, 98–108). It is fitting that such an important collection of his own letters and manuscripts should now be housed in the library in whose development he himself played such a dynamic role. He did not live to see the dramatic contraction of space forced upon his library in the later 1980s by the demand that the university make more economical use of its resources.

During the long phase of Larkin's life in Hull his literary reputation became firmly established with the publication by Faber and Faber of *The Whitsun Weddings* (1964) and *High Windows* (1974). He also produced a good deal of what he called 'required' (rather than inspired) writing. From 1961 to 1971 he was jazz critic of *The Daily Telegraph*, and his defences of traditional and attacks on 'progressive' jazz were collected in 1970 in the volume *All What Jazz*. In 1970–1 he spent two terms at All Souls College, Oxford, preparing *The Oxford Book of Twentieth Century English Verse*, which was published in 1973 to much critical controversy. Despite his growing fame he refused invitations to read his own poetry in public, and when he was offered the Laureateship following the death of Betjeman in 1984 he declined. He increasingly affected the pose of a recluse:

> My life is as simple as I can make it. Work all day, then cook, eat, wash up, telephone, hack writing, drink and television in the evenings. I almost never go out. I suppose

everyone tries to ignore the passing of time: some people by doing a lot, being in California one year and Japan the next; or there's my way – making every day and every year exactly the same. Probably neither works. (*RW*, 57–8)

He valued his geographical situation in Hull, since it made him relatively safe from intrusion. At this time the train-journey from London to Hull generally lasted five hours, and involved two changes of train (now it is direct and takes only three hours):

> I love all the Americans getting on to the train at King's Cross and thinking they're going to come and bother me, and then looking at the connections and deciding they'll go to Newcastle and bother Basil Bunting instead. Makes it harder for people to get at you. I think it's very sensible not to let people know what you're like. And Hull is an unpretentious place. There's not so much crap around as there would be in London, at least as I imagine it, or in some other university cities. (*RW*, 54–5)

He was insistent, however, in this same interview, that his association with Hull was not a matter of great profundity: 'I don't really notice where I live: as long as a few simple wants are satisfied – peace, quiet, warmth – I don't mind where I am . . . I very much feel the need to be on the periphery of things' (*RW*, 54–5). Larkin is frequently termed a provincial writer, but his neutral and detached attitude towards place is in fact the opposite of provincial.

In the BBC television programme of 1964, a faint, uneasy irony is detectable in Larkin's reaction to Betjeman's reading of his work as an enthusiastic celebration of his 'home'. As they sit among the overgrown monuments of Spring Bank Cemetery Betjeman says how easily he 'can understand' Larkin's liking for this place, going on to evoke a vision of the 'rich Hull merchants in big Italianate houses' who now lie in their 'death-beds' around them, and stating his preference for this graveyard's picturesque dereliction over the neatness and tidiness of a modern cemetery. Clearly impatient at Betjeman's imaginative bustle, Larkin breaks in to assert his own sensibility: 'I find that when I come here on a wet Sunday afternoon in December or something like that – when it isn't *at all* Romantic – it gets me into perspective, it gets my worries into perspective. And everything I write, I think, has the consciousness of approaching death in the background.' His interviewer responds appreciatively by misquoting 'Ambulances', Betjemanising the lugubriously measured Larkinesque phrase, 'So permanent and blank and true', into soft, rhetorical indulgence: 'So permanent and *black* and true' (with a heavy histrionic emphasis on 'black').

The *Monitor* programme begins with Betjeman gazing across the Humber from 'Tennyson's county' towards 'Philip Larkin's Hull'. But in fact Larkin's attitude towards Hull lacks the proprietorial flavour which Betjeman suggests. It has for instance none of the social familiarity which marks Betjeman's own vision of the Home Counties. In 'Here' the poet remains quite detached, by differences of taste and class, from the 'cut-price crowd' who inhabit the city, and the Holderness landscape at the end of the poem holds disembodied images of 'silence' standing like heat, of 'bluish neutral distance' and 'unfenced existence' (*CP*, 136-7), rather than any concrete realisation of the 'removed lives' of the local community. Nevertheless Larkin was prepared to acknowledge the creative value of a place like Hull to a poet like himself, even if he hedges this acknowledgement about with a profusion of cautious negatives: '. . . place cannot produce poems; it can only not prevent them, and Hull is good at that. It neither impresses or insists.' He saw Hull as being 'in the world, yet sufficiently on the edge of it to have a different resonance' ('A Place To Write'). It was in an attempt to preserve something of this different resonance that he lobbied unsuccessfully against the council's plans to tidy up the Spring Bank Cemetery in 1977 (Jean Hartley, 99).

One of Larkin's very few serious poetic mistakes was to yield to the pressure from friends and colleagues to 'insist' on Hull's behalf, and act as a public spokesman for the neglected region with which he had become identified. The result was 'Bridge for the Living', written in 1975 (*CP*, 203), a cantata celebrating the building of the Humber Bridge, a spectacular feat of engineering the main purpose of which was to encourage the growth of commerce and industry in the region, and thus dispel the precious isolation which Larkin so valued. Not surprisingly, the poet experienced some difficulty in producing a sufficient quantity of words for this celebratory pur- pose. Anthony Hedges, the composer, was originally commissioned to provide a forty-minute piece, which he estimated should require 350–400 lines of text (a previous setting by him of 250 lines having lasted thirty minutes). When Larkin's text arrived it contained only forty lines, and the commission had to be renegotiated down to twenty minutes.

Larkin admitted, in a letter to Hedges, to ambiguous feelings about the poem: 'the first part describes Hull's essential loneliness, and is descriptive and slow-moving, the second tries to feel cheerful about the ending of this loneliness through the agency of the bridge, and I suppose could be called celebratory'. Amis generously calls the result 'a splendid occasional poem' (1991, 64), but in fact it quite fails to escape the bad faith of its public origin. At times it affects a kind of cosy Betjemanese:

> Snow-thickened winter days are yet more still:
> Farms fold in fields, their single lamps come on,
> Tall church-towers parley, airily audible,
> Howden and Beverley, Hedon and Patrington . . .
>
> (CP, 203)

The facile euphony of 'airily audible' is excruciating in its coy playfulness. The final lines recycle a rhetorical pattern employed much earlier at the end of 'An Arundel Tomb':

> and to prove
> Our almost-instinct almost true:
> What will survive of us is love
> (CP, 111)

But the careful hesitancy of phrasing of the earlier lines is padded out in 'Bridge for the Living' into a wordy, repetitive declamation:

> Reaching for the world, as our lives do,
> As all lives do, reaching that we may give
> The best of what we are and hold as true:
> Always it is by bridges that we live.
> (CP, 204)

Verse which is written to be set to music can afford, perhaps, to be somewhat loose in texture. But this is merely banal. It is difficult not to feel that this poem would be more in place in *Required Writing* than in the *Collected Poems*.

A similar false note is struck by Larkin's solitary poetic venture into political commitment. About politics he had always been profoundly diffident ('I don't know anything at all about anything, and it[']s no use pretending I do'). As a rule he avoided wasting his creative energies on political themes. However, in 1969, when the radical ferment of the decade seemed to have carried all before it, he was goaded into breaking his otherwise sacrosanct principle never to be didactic, or make poetry '*do* things' (*RW*, 74). Encouraged by what others expected of him, he wrote two political poems. One of them, 'When the Russian tanks roll westward', is a single couplet of trochaic doggerel, attacking left-wing academics and students. It was published in a right-wing *Black Paper* on Education, and as this context suggests it is an ephemeral piece of 'required writing'.

'Homage to a Government', on the other hand, appeared in *High Windows*, and represents a more serious attempt to deal with a political issue in poetic terms. The poem regrets the British government's decision to close its base in Aden (now in the Republic of Yemen), as a cost-cutting exercise:

> Next year we are to bring the soldiers home
> For lack of money, and it is all right.
> Places they guarded, or kept orderly,
> Must guard themselves, and keep themselves orderly.
> We want the money for ourselves at home
> Instead of working. And this is all right.
>
> (*CP*, 171)

The repetition that it 'is all right' has a wan eloquence about it which is nicely ironic. But the poet's image of Britain's imperial role as a matter of keeping other places 'orderly' sounds thin and politically naïve. And the implication that the money saved by withdrawing the troops is intended to line the pockets of the work-shy is a gratuitous jibe which will only serve to alienate any reader not already in sympathy with the poem's attitudes. As Blake Morrison points out, 'financial motives are as involved in the posting of troops to colonies as they are in the withdrawal of them' (256). John Skinner has described the poem as an example of 'ambivalent discourse', observing that while the poet objects to the troops being brought home, he offers absolutely no positive reasons why they should be kept in Aden: no 'vision or conviction, not even self-interest or expediency'.

Skinner concludes that the 'feeble, apologetic voice' of the poet '*is* an embodiment of the precise reason why the troops *should* be brought home' (90).

Larkin seems himself to have been uneasily aware of these unintended ironies, and to have realised that this poem takes him out of his depth. His subsequent insistence that the work is not really political in intention has a desperate ring to it:

> Well, that's really history rather than politics. That poem has been quoted in several books as a kind of symbol of the British withdrawal from a world role. I don't mind troops being brought home if we'd decided this was the best thing all round, but to bring them home simply because we couldn't afford to keep them there seemed a dreadful humiliation. (*RW*, 52)

This is the only one of his poems whose supposed 'message' he felt it necessary to spell out and defend so explicitly. His attempt to argue that he was not, after all, venturing an opinion on anything as momentous as 'the British withdrawal from a world role' reveals his fundamental lack of political conviction, and – worse – his embarrassment at having forced his art. What can he mean by saying that the poem is a matter of 'history rather than politics'? And what does the phrase 'the best thing all round' signify in this context? Clearly Larkin does not know.

It is not here, but in his more casual remarks, that Larkin's political instincts find their most animated expression. Many anecdotes have gathered around the abrasive and entertaining persona of right-wing misanthrope which Larkin adopted in his later years. He used his increasing deafness to keep people at bay, and was rumoured to switch off his hearing-aid when he became bored, pretending that it was not working properly. Feeling himself embattled in an environment of left-wing academe where, particularly in the late 1960s and 1970s, student 'sit-ins' caused regular disruptions of the University's work, he delighted in outrageous statements intended to *épater les socialistes*. In 1976 I organised a petition asking the University Council to disinves: in companies whose South African subsidiaries paid their black workers wages below the official UN poverty-line. Larkin was asked in the bar one lunchtime what he thought of this colleague of his. He is reported to have replied 'He's performing a valuable function. It will be handy to have a complete list of all the pricks in the University.'

In the interviews of 1979 and 1982 this abrasive Tory Larkin finds his most accomplished literary expression:

> I've always been right-wing. It's difficult to say why, but not being a political thinker I suppose I identify the Right with certain virtues and the Left with certain vices. All very unfair, no doubt.
> *Which virtues and vices?*
> Well, thrift, hard work, reverence, desire to preserve – those are the virtues, in case you wondered: and on the other hand idleness, greed and treason. (*RW*, 52)

The asides form a rising emotional sequence: neutral and sincere-sounding ('It's difficult to say why'), then dismissive ('not being a political thinker'), and finally irascibly offhand ('All very unfair, no doubt'). Then as he gets further out of his depth he becomes edgily aggressive ('in case you wondered'), and, foundering by now, he turns up the volume of the rhetoric as if to cover his embarrassment, boldly accusing the Left of 'treason'. It may be suspected that, never having thought about politics in any serious way, he is reverting to the quirky, hectoring extremism of his father, which had had such an impact on him in his youth. The effect is consciously histrionic.

Larkin's first words in the *Observer* interview of 1979 were 'Actually, I like to think of myself as quite funny' (*RW*, 47), and a hint of fun, even of self-parody, seems evident in some of these political statements:

> *What do you think about Mrs Thatcher?*
> Oh, I adore Mrs Thatcher. At last politics makes sense to me, which it hasn't done since Stafford Cripps (I was very fond of him too). Recognizing that if you haven't got the money for something you can't have it – this is a concept that's vanished for many years. I'm delighted to see it surfacing again. (*RW*, 52)

The extravagant vocabulary of personal emotion ('adore', 'fond of'), is quite delicious, as is the preposterous comparison of the ascetic post-war Chancellor of the Exchequer, Cripps, architect of rationing and austerity, with the millionaire's wife who was to preside over the largest expansion of personal credit in Britain's history (though, to be fair, Larkin was not to know that in 1979). It is pertinent here, if perhaps merciless, to note that Larkin's enthusiasm for the principle that 'if you haven't got the money for something you can't have it' had not always been so intense. The letters reveal that he had stolen books on at least three occasions. In 1941 he stole a copy of *The Senior Commoner* by Julian Hall from Earlsdon Public Library in Coventry (24.ix.41), and a short time afterwards, when he was 19, he took an edition of Blake from a shop in Oxford: 'By the way, I *stole* the Nonesuch Blake and am expecting the police to call for me any minute. It is a beautiful 15/- book and just what I want. But I ain't goin' there no more. No sah!' (23.xii.41). Ten years later, at the age of 28, he stole a novel by Llewellyn Powys from a local library in Belfast (8.v.51).

The mature Larkin possesses no harmoniously consistent system of 'conservative' views covering art and morality. 'Irresponsibility' offends him only when it expresses itself in bad art. He dismisses the 'drop-out' writers of the 1950s with a stern contempt: 'there seems little new in the Beat Generation unless it is a new degree of hysteria in art or irresponsibility in life' (*RW*, 119). But he is indulgent to the Victorian 'drop-out' Francis Thompson, who was prepared to suffer in the service of his muse: 'If he was work-shy, he was ready to pay the price; and in those days that meant hunger and homelessness, not a dainty progression from foundation to fellowship over the safety net of national assistance' (*RW*, 121). 'And whose heart would not be softened', Larkin adds, by Thompson's poetry? Similarly, the rejection of the sinecure of a librarianship by the Georgian poet and 'super-tramp' W. H. Davies fills him with envious admiration:

> 'They wanted me to work,' Davies said years later in relating his rejection of this ignoble proposal. 'I have never worked in my life.' There was nothing for it, the friends realized, but a Civil List pension. (*RW*, 164)

It is wholly characteristic that, when asked whether he had ever tried consciousness-expanding drugs, Larkin replied not with a moral tirade against the irresponsible youth of today, but by referring to the drug most in use by his own generation: 'No, though of course my generation are drinkers. Not druggers' (*RW*, 71).

On reaching the age of 50 in 1972 Larkin felt despairingly certain that his inspiration was fading. Then in 1974, after eighteen years in his flat on the edge of Pearson Park, he bought a house nearer to the university. All who knew him seem to concur with the verdict that 'This move was traumatic . . . he never enjoyed in the new house the tranquillity and inspiration he had found in the flat where he had spent the happiest and most creatively successful period of his life' (Brennan, 36). During his last decade his increasing deafness also served to drive him back into himself. Despite his assertions of bachelor independence, as he had grown older Philip's relationship with Monica Jones had come increasingly to approximate to the domestic routines and dependencies of marriage. Then, in the early 1980s, some time after she had retired from Leicester University she suffered a bad attack of shingles and Philip brought her to Hull to recuperate. In the event she remained with him. Her health deteriorated further, and during his final years Larkin's constant excuse for refusing social invitations was that he must stay in to look after her:

> 27 Dec 1983
> . . . The fact is that M really isn't up to 'going out' in the evenings, and I shouldn't like to desert her on New Year's Eve, which we have been in the habit of spending together . . . With all good wishes for this ominous New Year – personally I have no great hopes. (Unpublished letter)

Ironically, it was he who died first, of cancer, on 2 December 1985, at the same age as his father, 63. He anticipated his approaching death with fatalism, withdrawing into himself, out of a wish, as he put it, not to 'scare' others. His lifelong friend Kingsley Amis, learning that he was dying, expressed the desire to come to Hull to see him one last time. But Larkin discouraged him.

At the age of 18 Larkin had wandered round a graveyard, reading epitaphs:

> One stone said 'In loving remembrance of Philip Larkin: In the midst of life we are in death.' Major think. I reeled away conscious of a desire to vomit into a homburg hat. (9.xii.40)

Throughout his life he dreaded death. It was his sense of death's pitiless finality – 'All we have done not mattering' (*CP*, 59) – which made life so precious to him and gave intensity to his poetry. 'The ultimate joy is to be alive, in the flesh. Shake that thing' (23.vi.41). He knew that 'nothing contravenes/The coming dark' (*CP*, 193), and therefore anticipated no afterlife. Religion was for him a touching self-delusion, a 'vast moth-eaten musical brocade/Created to pretend we never die' (*CP*, 208). His aesthetic feeling for such delusion, however, together with his lifelong conservatism, led him to direct that he should be buried according to the poetic rites of the Church of England, rather than the prose of a secular cremation. The clergyman who gave the address at his funeral called him a 'reluctant disbeliever', which is perhaps not a wholly inaccurate choice of words. However he was never an 'earnest seeker after truth', and the unflinching scepticism of poems such as 'Church Going' and 'An Arundel Tomb' is far indeed from the sentimental religiosity for which it is sometimes mistaken. The words which Monica Jones chose for his gravestone exclude piety and delusion, leaving only the art to which he had devoted his life:

PHILIP LARKIN
1922–1985
WRITER

2

Diffused Poetry

THE NOVELS

I n an early letter to Sutton the nineteen-year-old Larkin accurately predicted the shape of his artistic career:

> I have in my head shadowy plans for a novel – nothing to get excited about, but I feel I should try before I finally sprout wings and turn into a poet dashing forward like a Hussar . . . If I could do it as I imagine it, it would be a really poetic novel. (5.iii.42)

The glancing reference to Auden's poem 'The Novelist' (in the image of the poet as dashing 'hussar') serves only to draw attention to the difference between Larkin's 'poetic' concept of the novel and the more familiar notion of the older poet. Auden's novelist 'Must struggle out of his boyish gift and learn/ How to be plain and awkward'. Larkin's career reverses this progression, moving from the responsibilities of prose to the self-expression of lyric poetry. Moreover, his conception of the novel is quite unlike Auden's. He shows little interest in the moral omnivorousness which Auden attributes to his novelist:

> he must
> Become the whole of boredom, subject to
> Vulgar complaints like love, among the Just

Be just, among the Filthy filthy too,
And in his own weak person, if he can,
Dully put up with all the wrongs of Man.

Such moral purpose and social commitment do not concern Larkin. In one of his earliest letters to Sutton he declared roundly, 'A novel should be a diffused poem' (28.xii.40), and on completing the first draft of *Jill*, he proudly compared it with George Moore's 'real prose poem' *Esther Waters* (8.ii.44).

The natural models for the kind of novel Larkin wished to write were the works of Virginia Woolf. In an early letter he expressed intense admiration for Woolf's most experimentally poetic novel, *The Waves*, and while he was at work on *A Girl in Winter* he told Sutton 'If I write like anybody it is like Virginia Woolf – but much better, or it will be' (14.ix.44). However, his poetic conception of the novel is not consistent. Though he emulates Woolf, and also Katherine Mansfield, in his prose style, he does not follow them in formal innovation. Indeed his novels rely somewhat mechanically on social-realist characterisation and plotted incident. The influence of his friend, the future novelist Kingsley Amis, was no doubt a factor here. But more important seems to have been his fixation with D. H. Lawrence. Larkin does not directly imitate Lawrence, whom he considered 'too far above me to be any use to me' (17.iv.44). But the example of Lawrence's unforced blend of social realism and poetic symbolism seems to have inhibited him from moving to the freer, more subjective artistic form which might have been expected to follow from his 'diffused poem' conception of the novel.

It would not be too difficult, for instance, to imagine the Larkin of the Sutton letters rejecting plot and characterisation in the usual sense, and composing a masterpiece in the manner of Stevie Smith's *Novel on Yellow Paper*. But instead, what troubles him, as he composes *Jill*, is the comparison with 'real life' and with the classic realism of early Lawrence: 'But it's very tiny and thin really, when put up against real life, or *Sons and Lovers*. That book's a winder, as Morel would say. It extracts the urine from any given would-be writer. When I look at it in the bookcase, I can see it *breathing*, very slightly' (29.xii.43). It is tempting to detect a gender conflict in these influences (Lawrence and Amis versus Woolf and Mansfield), particularly in view of the importance of female centres of consciousness in both Larkin's completed novels. It is certainly true that the most free-flowing poetic elements in these works are generated by the women characters, 'Jill' and Katherine, while the brutal closures which terminate them are imposed on the women by the men: Kemp, Warner, Anstey and Robin. The result is an uneasy marriage of poetry and realism which never achieves formal conviction.

Larkin's poetic conception of the novel explains why his career as a novelist had to run its course before his career as a major poet could begin. During the time that he considered himself primarily a novelist he wrote only derivative and immature poetry, because his best poetry found its way into his prose. The poems of *The North Ship* (1945), as he commented himself, are less original than the poetic novels he wrote at the same period. Both his published novels were completed by 1945; the earliest poems which Thwaite considers worthy of inclusion in the main body of the *Collected Poems* date from 1946. Though Larkin continued to work on his third novel until about the time of his move to Belfast in 1950, and even began work on a fourth, no projected titles are ever mentioned in his letters to Sutton. Almost against his will Larkin found himself turning to poetry instead. He complained in a letter: 'I can write poems now and again *because I want to write novels so badly*' (20.v.50). A shift from the 'over-sized poems' of his novels (in Hamilton, 75) to undiffused poems was the natural solution.

JILL

When the story that was to become *Jill* first appears in the letters it seems peculiarly ambiguous:

> It could lengthen into a novel, if I could ever do it. It concerns a very poor young man who goes to Oxford who is exceptionally nervous and rather feminine, who is forced to share a room with his exact antithesis. As a result of adverse conditions, and also of telling his room-mate that he had a sister a year younger than himself (or two or three years) – which is untrue – he begins to evolve a complicated sexless daydream about an imaginary sister, who serves as a nucleus for a dream-life. Then he meets a girl who is exactly like this imaginary sister (the sister aspect having by now changed into rather a more emotional relationship) and the rest of the

story, in action and in a long dream, serves to disillusion
him completely. It's a jolly good story, whatever it sounds
like thus barely expressed, and interests me greatly.
(10.viii.43)

It is not immediately apparent what it is that 'interests' Larkin so
greatly about this story. Clearly it is not its moral and social content,
which remains quite obscure. Is this 'rather feminine' young man's
disillusionment with his fantasies of girlhood to be seen as an
awakening to harsh 'reality', or is the story – as Larkin's defensive
but defiant tone suggests – simply a vehicle for the author's own
'dream'? In his next letter to Sutton, Larkin invokes the dialect of a
D. H. Lawrence character to mock his tale's failure to engage with
reality. His language is aggressively masculine:

The long story I sent you the plot of displeases me – about
the Oxford lad. Its got no guts, no earth. Wheer keeps tha
ba's, lad? I long to write a story where there's a lot of
fighting and raping and money-making – not just endless,
over-subtle conversations, like the ones I do at present.
(16.viii.43)

Paradoxically however he proposes to transcend the 'Oxford Novel'
tradition, not by the introduction of 'fighting and raping and money-
making' but by emulating the exquisite style of Katherine
Mansfield, whose stories and journals he was constantly rereading at
the time. He hopes to write 'with such a double-distilled purity of
essence-of-Mansfield – that suddenly the reader will think "This
isn't a novel about Oxford – it's a novel" ' (30.ix.43).

These contradictions are carried through unresolved into the
finished work. Ostensibly the novel shows a working-class boy
receiving bitter lessons in maturity against a background of class
conflict and war. But this realistic story is merely the context for the
more imaginatively engrossing 'diffused poem' of Kemp's fantasies
and dreams. The most successful artistic element in the novel is the
poetic evocation of the texture of Kemp's consciousness, and Larkin
finds it difficult to breathe any life into the realistic analysis of the
psychological and social effects of the British class system in which
this poetic evocation is situated. Kemp's initial impressions of
Oxford, for instance, insistently signal his social origin. He is

unaware that 'Town' means London (27), and impressed that his room in college 'was bigger than any in his own house' (28). His room-mate's shaving lotion and talcum powder are unknown exotic substances to him (34). Then the 'flashback' concerning Kemp's schoolteacher gives the novel an awkward turn. After a burst of enthusiastic encouragement of his promising pupil, Mr Crouch finds himself losing interest in a boy whose 'character was almost purely negative . . . There was no fun in teaching so matter-of-fact a mind' (79). Larkin shows little concern to correct Mr Crouch's verdict here, and the reader may suspect that the young author himself has also begun to find his protagonist somewhat boring. Throughout the novel Kemp's role continues to shift uneasily between detached poetic sensibility and almost contemptibly pathetic 'scholarship-boy'.

In his later comments on the novel Larkin disclaimed any interest in the 'displaced working class hero', and was earnest to deny that *Jill* had anything in common with the 'Movement' and 'Angry Young Man' novels which followed it in the 1950s (by Amis, Wain and Braine), in which class conflict and jealousies are dramatised in terms of a love-affair between a working-class young man and a middle-class girl. '*Jill* has none of the political overtones of that *genre*' he said, and insisted that he had made Kemp of a lower class than himself not because he wished to convey any social message, but for contingent and subjective reasons: 'John's being working-class was a kind of equivalent of my stammer, a built-in handicap to put him one down' (*RW*, 63). He even argued preposterously that his novel reflected the social egalitarianism of the war period: 'In 1940 our impulse was still to minimize social differences rather than exaggerate them. My hero's background, though an integral part of the story, was not what the story was about' (*RW*, 17). In fact, far from reflecting the classlessness of the war period, the novel is an unquestioning expression of class prejudice. The minor characters are all stereotypes, arranged in the simplest diagram of class antagonisms: on the one hand Chris Warner, the public-school 'hearty' of whom Kemp is jealous; on the other Whitbread, a philistine version of Kemp's own 'scholarship-boy' self, of whom he is contemptuous. Kemp remains throughout a slave to Warner's public-school glamour and sexual ease: 'When he looked at them both [Warner and Elizabeth], he felt like a waiter in an expensive restaurant. Their friendliness to him was like the tips they would give a waiter' (110). All the women in the novel, Elizabeth, Gillian, Warner's glamorous mother, naturally belong to Warner.

The character of Whitbread – and to a degree also of Kemp himself – originated, as Larkin tells us in the 1963 introduction, in the 'Yorkshire scholar' whom he and his tutorial mate Normal Iles invented, 'a character embodying many of our prejudices' (*RW*, 19), whose 'flat rapacious tones' they would imitate as they walked to classes: 'You're gettin' the best education in the land, lad.' 'Ay, but you must cut your coat according to your cloth.' 'Had tea wi't' Dean on Sunday – I showed him I'd been reading his book.' 'Never lose a chance to make a good impression' (*RW*, 19). In the novel the humour is less secure, the broad accent is toned down, and the character is reduced to the merest reflex of class prejudice:

> He had a pale stubbly head, queerly like a dormouse, and thick steel-rimmed spectacles: he spoke with a flat York-shire accent that made John suppose wrongly that he had a sense of humour. John could tell by his clothes that he was not well-off, and he remembered a phrase from one of his mother's letters (it was still in his pocket) that said that she hoped he had made some friends 'of his own standing'. With a gust of indignation he realized that she meant people like Whitbread. (51)

The phrase 'queerly like a dormouse' seems to promise Lawrentian intensities. But in fact the characterisation is a simple matter of steel-rimmed spectacles, shabby clothes, flat accent and bad manners: 'Whitbread's eagerness was embarrassing: it was like watching a man scouring his plate with a piece of bread' (53). Here, as elsewhere, it is the shallow parameters of middle-class taste which determine the novel's characterisation.

A comparison with Amis's *Lucky Jim*, published in 1954, nine years after *Jill*, and dedicated to Larkin, shows how much more successful this aspect of his novel might have been had Larkin's social attitudes been more flexible and his imagination less poetic. Amis's first novel had been a long time in gestation and was originally based on his impression of Larkin's life in Leicester in the late 1940s. The relationship between Jim and Margaret is apparently Amis's caricature of that between Philip and Monica Jones at this period. Given the close association between the two writers, the similarities between *Jill* and *Lucky Jim* are not surprising, though Amis's novel is clearly a more assured work. Both novels focus on the young protagonist's pursuit of a girl who is apparently out of their class. Both protagonists are in awe of a middle-class rival (Warner, Bertrand) who has a prior claim on the desired girl. Both novels reach an embarrassing climax focusing on the protagonist's public drunkenness. There are many minor parallels: Dixon's destruction of the insurance policies piled on Johns's desk for instance echoes Kemp's wrecking of Whitbread's room in *Jill*. Some of these similarities could well be the result of Larkin's influence on Amis, or even of his collaboration in the composition of Amis's novel, about which he was later rather vague: 'Well, it's all so long ago, it's hard to remember . . . I said, Cut this, cut that, let's have more of the other . . .' (*RW*, 59).

But, however extensive the collaboration, these parallels only serve to point up how utterly different Amis's novel is from Larkin's. Amis's protagonist, Dixon, for example, with his 'flat northern voice' (Ch. 1) is another version of the 'Yorkshire scholar' of their undergraduate jokes, and at the beginning of the novel a similar mixture of sympathy and contempt can be detected in Amis's approach to his protagonist as in Larkin's to his. But Amis's attitudes to class are more kinetic, and his novelistic instinct soon leads him into an empathy with his character's embarrassments which makes Dixon a far more human creation than Kemp. To put it crudely, the reader of *Lucky Jim* is invited actively to share Jim's desire to get the unattainable girl and the money. Without this 'gut' response the book's narrative of trivial social encounters would become tedious and lame. On the other hand, unlike Larkin's, Amis's novel has no dimension beyond the social: nothing purely aesthetic or poetic. In Amis's world everything is priced in terms of money, sex and power. There are no other categories of significance. Dixon's social aspirations are clear and simple, while Kemp's are unreal and uninteresting. Kemp desires nothing as material as the girl and the money, and creates in his fantasy of 'Jill' an imaginative world undefinable in terms of sexual or financial success.

With the partial exception of Margaret, Amis's supporting characters are as stereotyped and flat as Larkin's. But, whereas in *Jill* these characters remain largely static, in *Lucky Jim* they are brought to garish life by the plot. The antics of Amis's characters give them a far greater appeal than those of Larkin. The various Welches stand, grotesque and threatening, between the protagonist and his attainment of the sex and the money which he so acutely desires. Consequently the plot of Amis's novel becomes a riveting and suspenseful series of comic delays. Amis would never create a character like Whitbread, who performs no plot function whatsoever. When one of Larkin's characters does apparently fulfil something of the function of one of Amis's grotesques, the effect is halfhearted, as though the author cannot really be bothered with such tricks of the novelistic trade. For instance the enumeration of Kemp's careful preparations for Gillian's tea-time visit seems intended to build up suspense. And, sure enough, his plans are cruelly thwarted by Elizabeth, who unexpectedly arrives instead of Gillian to warn him off. But, since Kemp's intentions in relation to Gillian are so undefined, the reader feels little sense of drama at this point. Instead, the focus falls on the state of the protagonist's mind, as he plunges from elation to despair. Amis would not waste so splendid an opportunity to 'get his readers going'. His protagonist would at once start planning how to defeat Elizabeth who, because of her interference, would appear wholly odious. The reader would already be anticipating the coming battle of the sexes with relish. In the crudest terms *Lucky Jim* is 'a good read'; *Jill* is not.

The contrast between the novelists is most striking in their attitudes towards collective social experience. The sense of national, class and cultural solidarity is very important in Amis's work. He seems in retrospect 'typical' of a generation. Like so many young men of his time he served in the army, and his early work expresses the feelings of the ex-conscript, increasingly resentful of the restraints of post-war austerity. His is a psychology of dogged conformism punctuated by outbursts of anarchy. The abolition of National Service in 1961 marks an important watershed between this guilt-ridden, conservative generation of the 1940s and 1950s and the permissive children of the 1960s. *Lucky Jim* is also rich in the dated 'feel' of the fifties, in social nuance and physical landscape. It even tells its readers the amount of change a customer would get from half-a-crown after buying two pints of beer in 1954. Such 'period' richness scarcely features in Larkin's work. To some extent this may result from the different nature of Larkin's experience. He had remained on the sidelines, avoiding the army and later insulated in the sedentary security of his librarianship. But the difference is also a more organically aesthetic one. When, in the 1963 introduction, he

wrote about the atmosphere of Oxford in the early 1940s, he only
served to emphasise how little *Jill* appears in this light, as a record or
a celebration of its time. The Oxford of *Jill* is too personal and
poetically internalised to prompt the delighted recognition with
which older readers still greet *Lucky Jim*.

As a realistic novel, then, *Jill* appears narrow and disappointing.
As a 'diffused poem', however, it is, for all its immaturities, original
and occasionally beautiful. As a poetic creation Kemp is not a study
in social problems, but a lyric projection of the young author
himself:

> His face was thin, and perhaps strained; the expression
> round his mouth was ready to become taut, and a small
> frown lingered on his forehead. His whole appearance
> lacked luxuriance. Only his silky hair, as soft as seeding
> thistle, gave him an air of beauty. (21)

Whenever Larkin concentrates single-mindedly on realising the
texture of Kemp's consciousness, his loneliness and elations, the
writing becomes assured and transparent:

> Looking up from the stone enclosure, he could see the sky
> full of innumerable trembling stars, and all he could hear
> was extravagant sounds at a distance – drunken howling
> from a far street, something that might have been a revolver
> shot, and, from somewhere in the College itself, the hysteri-
> cal crying of a jazz record. Close to all was quiet: the
> slightest of winds breathed over the grass and around the
> stone pillars, while from the Master's garden came the
> restless sound of trees. He wondered if a time would ever
> come when these things would assure him and seem
> pleasant. (40)

Here Kemp's social ineffectiveness is transformed into a rare ego-
less detachment. Some of the most poetic passages in the novel
express a sense of obliteration of an almost spiritual intensity: 'A
dismal melancholy was beginning to expand inside him, a great
loneliness . . . He looked around the room for evidence of his own
presence, but found very little' (37).

As Kingsley Amis has revealed, the germ from which the novel

grew was the schoolgirl 'Willow Gables fantasy', which, in the final
version, is the young protagonist's first attempt to escape from his
loneliness into a world of imagination. According to Amis this
episode had originally 'come to independent life as a kind of pastiche
of schoolgirl stories'. Amis adds: 'When the book finally appeared I
was amazed at the skill that half concealed the utter incongruity of
that episode with the rest of the material' (1982, 27). As David
Timms has pointed out, it is quite implausible that a working-class
boy like Kemp, who does not even know what talcum powder or
shaving-lotion are, should be able to parody the jargon of a girl's
boarding school so brilliantly (Timms 1973/4ii, 161). The imaginative confidence and elaboration of the writing are Larkin's rather
than Kemp's:

> TUESDAY. Oh, a horrid day. Horrid and hateful! Now the
> novelty's worn off (and it wears off damned quickly in these
> days) I'm getting to hate it as much as ever. All my kirbi-
> grips had vanished for a start this morning (yes, and WHO
> took them?), so what with searching for them and trying to
> find a slide, I hadn't time to get my hymn-book before
> prayers – and of course the Badger had to choose today to
> inspect them, as she said she'd seen too many girls sharing
> recently. I suppose she thinks I *like* sharing with Molly.
> (149)

As the product of the imagination of a young author in his early
twenties this element of the book is rather strange. One explanation
could be that it is an unusual kind of pornography. Despite, or rather
because of, their 'complicated sexless' quality, 'Jill's' letters and
diary might be interpreted as a strenuously displaced sublimation of
Kemp's (Larkin's) sexual desires: a kind of ultra-refined psychological transvestism. In his Introduction to the American edition of
1976 Larkin explains that Reginald Caton of the Fortune Press, who
published the book, 'divided his publishing activity between poetry
and what then passed for pornography' (*RW*, 25–6), and he jokes
that Kingsley Amis once saw *Jill* on a bookshop shelf 'between
Naked and Unashamed and *High-Heeled Yvonne*' (*RW*, 24). In his
Memoirs Amis refers to the novel's 'super-soft porn undertones'
(1991, 55), and certainly its elaborately displaced fiction-within-a-
fiction – the author portraying a hypersensitive Oxford under-

graduate impersonating his pre-sexual 'sister' – must offer a degree of titillation to some readers.

But the poetic level of the novel rises above a mere case study of Kemp's (Larkin's) adolescent sexual psychology. Kemp's enjoyment of his fantasy has a detached and aesthetic quality which makes his 'Jill' as much a work of art as a symptom of repression. Kemp feels that he has discovered something already there, rather than having invented something: '. . . each minute seemed to clarify her, as if the picture of her had been stacked away waiting in his mind, covered with dust, until this should happen' (135–6). This is clearly the process of poetic creation which Larkin describes in his letters to Sutton. It is 'like trying to remember a tune you've forgotten' (28.xii.40), or uncovering a pre-existent entity: 'You see, there's only *one* version of any poem: the "writing" of it is the discovering of that one version' (22.ix.44). In this perspective the novel concerns the familiar theme of Life versus Art. Indeed, despite his later dismissal of the 'common myth-kitty' of poetic symbols, *Jill* is in fact an easily legible version of the ancient Pygmalion myth. Pygmalion creates a statue of a beautiful woman, with which he falls in love so intensely that it comes to life. Keats saw artistic creation in terms of the similar myth of Adam dreaming of Eve: 'He awoke and found it true.'

It is this which explains Kemp's exhilarated sense of achievement as he begins to assert the reality of his literary creation by actually sending letters to his dream-figment. On the level of sober realism the reader might expect to feel pity at these signs of Kemp's mental derangement, or at least his inane silliness. Instead, Larkin succeeds in conveying the exaltation of the artist in the act of selfless creation:

> He was trembling when he dropped it into a pillar-box, and leant against the wall a moment, filled with exultation at the idea of thus speaking with nothingness. He envisaged the envelope wandering around England, collecting pencilled scribbles of suggestions on the front and back until, perhaps a year or more hence, it came to rest in some dusty corner of a dead-letter office. How many years would it stay there? Till he, perhaps, had changed out of all knowing.
>
> He must write again, write dozens of them: dozens of letters to Miss Jill Bradley must wander through the postal service. (131–2)

Kemp is quite aware that he is 'speaking with nothingness'. But this is precisely what excites him. His letter-writing offers him the purest aesthetic activity, for its own sake. It offers escape from the chaos of the real world; it annuls his inadequate social self. But he cannot maintain this fine-spun dream for long. The appearance of a real Jill, or rather Gillian (reality is ominously out of focus with his fantasy) returns the hard-won freedom of his imagination to the bondage of his adolescent sexual desires. Also, since Gillian turns out to be the cousin of Elizabeth, Warner's girlfriend, Kemp's most effective escape from Warner is ironically transformed into yet another attribute of Warner's social superiority. The result is disaster, as crude reality superimposes itself on his beautiful dream. He gets drunk, and kisses Gillian as she leaves a college party, only to be beaten up and thrown into a fountain by Warner's hearties.

This reading apparently returns the novel to the level of moral and psychological realism. The book offers, so it seems, a didactic lesson on reality and illusion in the familiar terms of male disillusion with romanticised femininity. But this version is misleading. The arraignment of Kemp's (or Larkin's) aestheticism by prosaic 'reality' is severely compromised by the novel's poetry. In the end the author himself prefers dream to reality and Kemp learns no more salutary lesson than does Lycius at the end of Keats's 'Lamia'. As a 'diffused poem' the world of the novel remains enclosed within the sensibility of its poetic protagonist. Even the most momentous 'objective' realities in the book become imaginatively real only in their relation to Kemp's state of mind. This is startlingly illustrated by what should, by all normal novelistic criteria, be Kemp's sternest lesson in 'reality', namely his visit to his bombed home town (a version of Larkin's own Coventry). Here, if anywhere, is an experience to shock Kemp out of his escapist fantasy, and to break the spell of his hermetic aestheticism. The author virtually promises as much: 'As the train left Oxford John had a pang of regret and also of fear, because he seemed to be leaving a region of unreality and insubstantial pain for the real world where he could really be hurt' (211).

But in the event the test does not materialise. No human victims are seen, no physical or mental suffering. The only person Kemp meets is a casual acquaintance, 'a boy who had been at school with him' (212). His own home is untouched by the bombs, and his family is safe in Preston. Kemp and the reader are thus left free to roam a devastated landscape, drinking in poignant visual impressions:

'. . . broken bricks, lurching floors and laths sticking out like delicate broken bones . . .' (212). 'The moon, by day a thin pith-coloured segment, hung brilliantly in the sky, spilling its light down on to the skeletons of roofs, blank walls and piles of masonry that undulated like a frozen sea. It had never seemed so bright' (215). Larkin's protagonist then returns to Oxford busily converting the literal destruction he has just seen into a metaphor of imaginative release from his oppressive background:

> he saw once again the scarecrow buildings, the streets half heaved-up by detonations, the candlelit bar. It no longer seemed meaningless: struggling awake again, rubbing his eyes with chilled hands, he thought it represented the end of his use for the place. It meant no more to him now, and so it was destroyed: it seemed symbolic, a kind of annulling of his childhood. The thought excited him. It was as if he had been told: all the past is cancelled: all the suffering connected with that town, all your childhood, is wiped out. Now there is a fresh start for you: you are no longer governed by what has gone before. (219)

The Blitz is readily transmuted into an intense, poetic symbol of the protagonist's creative 'fresh start'. For Larkin the war is not a common experience bringing people together in the solidarity of shared fear and grief, as Louis MacNeice naturally depicts it in poems like 'Hiatus' and 'Aftermath'. For the author of *Jill* the war is meaningful only when it has been internalised into a subjective symbol. Otherwise it is 'meaningless'. As a novel concerned with the conflict between 'unreality' and the 'real world', *Jill* is confused and incoherent; as a lyrical evocation of the protagonist's (or author's) youthful fantasies and disillusionments, it possesses a peculiar power.

A GIRL IN WINTER

A Girl in Winter was written while Larkin was librarian in Wellington, Shropshire, and completed on 9 August 1945. In an interview of 1982 he said that he always thought of it as *The Kingdom of Winter*, its original, and preferable, title. *The Kingdom of Winter* is more abstract, and indicates the poetic intensity and bleakness of the book better than *A Girl in Winter*, which conveys misleading hints of sentiment and romance. In the same interview Larkin recollects feeling 'pretty low' during its composition (*RW*, 63), a recollection confirmed by the Sutton letters: 'I find little exaltation in writing it, but just keep carefully at it, hoping for the best. I haven't written a poem for AGES – I am fundamentally a prose writah' (3.v.45).

The novel's central dream/reality conflict is similar to that in *Jill*, but is more effectively embodied in the novel's form: three sections moving from real present to dream past and back again. It is this larger emotional structure which remains in the reader's memory rather than the convolutions of the plot. The protagonist, Katherine Lind, a refugee from Europe, works in the library of a Midland town under the unpleasant regime of the librarian, Mr Anstey, whose name, appropriately enough, is a perfunctory anagram of 'nasty' (Timms 1973/4 ii, 161). In the first section she is sent to the dentist with one of the junior librarians, Miss Green, who has a toothache. Calling at a chemist's shop on the way she picks up someone else's handbag in mistake for Miss Green's and, trying to discover its owner, finds a letter inside it addressed to a Miss V. Parbury in the handwriting of Mr Anstey. But this trivial plot elaboration scarcely rivets the reader's attention. Much more important to the effect of the opening section is Katherine's rapt preoccupation, as she traverses the bitter winter landscape, clenched against the cold. She insulates herself from the shabby provincial world around her partly by an inner rejection of its sordidness, and partly by the eager expectation of a letter from an English friend, Robin Fennel. Her discovery of Mr Anstey's letter to Miss Parbury coincides with the arrival of a letter from Robin, now a soldier in the army, promising to visit her that very afternoon.

The second section of the novel concerns Katherine's recollections of the holiday she spent some years before with the Fennels in their house in the country. A pen-friend arrangement at her school had led to an invitation from Robin's sister, and during the summer holiday the sixteen-year-old schoolgirl had developed a romantic attachment to her reserved young host. Her emotion seems as much an effect of the landscape and foreign context as of real attachment:

> The water was the colour of pewter, for the afterglow had
> faded rapidly and left a quality of light that resembled early

dawn. It had drawn off the brightness from the meadows
and stubble-fields, that were now tarnished silver and pale
yellow, and the shadows were slowly mixing with the mist.
In this way the edges of her emotions had blurred, and they
now overlaid each other like twin planes of water running
over wet sand, the last expenditure of succeeding waves.
There was no longer any discord in them: she felt at peace.
　'Robin, what is this river called?' she asked after a while.
　'Why, the Thames, of course.' (172)

The relaxed summer atmosphere, boldly contrasted with the kingdom of winter of the first section, is described in language of delicate
insubstantiality, conveying both the beauty and the fragility of this
idyll. During the catastrophes of the war Katherine has treasured
this English dream, and after coming back to England she has
written to Jane, Robin's sister: hence Robin's approaching visit.

　Initially however the third section of the book returns to the
unfinished sub-plot of Mr Anstey and Miss Parbury. Dis-
encumbered of Miss Green after the visit to the dentist, and finding
it too late to return to her morning's work, Katherine suddenly feels
shy of the imminent arrival of Robin, and decides to avoid him by
seeking out Miss Parbury to return the handbag. On the way she
cannot resist reading Mr Anstey's letter, which reveals that he is
trying to persuade this woman to put her mother into a nursing
home so that they can be married. Veronica Parbury turns out to be a
painfully pathetic figure, loyally tending her bedridden mother in a
domestic environment of Graham Greene-like drabness: 'there were
no books in the room except a small shelf in the window, and this
was filled with dreary rubbish, such as a Holiday Haunts for 1928.
This gave the room a slack, soulless air. Through the window she
could see a depressing yard, with a bucket standing in the snow, and
a high wall' (193).

　When Katherine returns to the library late in the afternoon Mr
Anstey calls her into his office to complain about her attitude to her
work, and to tell her that a telephoned telegram has arrived in which
Robin has cancelled his visit. Despite having earlier sought to avoid a
meeting with Robin, Katherine is now desolate that he has not come,
and in response to Mr Anstey's masculine bluster she dramatically
resigns her job and throws his pathetic relationship with Miss
Parbury in his face:

'Oh, shut up with your advice, shut up. I don't want it, you
bore me stiff with such things.' She drew a deep breath to
stop herself panting. 'Keep it. Keep it for your Miss Greens
and Miss Feathers and your silly Veronica Parbury,' drawl-
ing out the last three words with an exaggerated foreign
accent she had learned annoyed people. (210)

She returns to her flat at the end of the day to find that Robin has
arrived after all, no longer the figment of her dream but a commonplace young soldier, drunk and importunate. Her delicate idyll is
shattered and at the end of the novel, beaten down by the day's
disasters, she submits wearily to his sexual demands, drifting to sleep
in a nihilistic state of disillusion, a resigned subject of the kingdom of
winter, dreaming of icebergs, annihilation and darkness.

This summary of the events of the novel gives a misleading
prominence to its inconclusive and mechanically overcomplicated
plot. In fact Mr Anstey appears only in two brief scenes, Miss
Parbury in one, and the reader does not learn enough to become
interested in either of them. They remain symbols of sterility and
sordidness. The very artistic awkwardness of the letter-in-the-
handbag plot-device seems to express their creator's irritation with
the characters. The imaginative effect of the novel is created not by
plot or characterisation, but by image and texture, and by the broad
rhythm of its three-part structure. Though Larkin had seen the
problem with his first novel as its lack of 'guts' or 'earth', his artistic
instinct seems to have driven him in his second novel even further
into poetic purity and attenuation. In artistic terms his instinct was
clearly sound. *A Girl in Winter* resolves most of the problems of *Jill*
by marginalising social realism even further and by giving fuller play
to the poetry.

The most important factor in the relatively greater poetic coher-
ence of the second novel is its centre of consciousness, Katherine.
The confusions which attended the portrayal of Kemp, an English
man, are dispelled now that the centre of consciousness is a foreign
woman. Kemp was a muddled mixture of social realism and poetic
sensibility: a 'rather feminine' working-class youth, fantasising
about kirbi-grips and schoolgirl slang in a somewhat implausible
attempt to compensate for his social inadequacies. Katherine is, in
contrast, a fundamentally poetic creation. As a foreigner, she is, like
the working-class Kemp, lonely and out of place, but since she is a

war refugee, her loneliness requires no detailed social explanation, and remains a disembodied, symbolic element. Despite his later declaration of his 'hatred of abroad' (*RW* 47), Larkin makes Katherine's foreignness into a strangely positive element in her presentation. It, as it were, purifies her – and through her Larkin's vision of England – of the tangle of social prejudices and resentments of his own insider's perspective. The form of her Christian name suggests that she is French or Belgian, rather than Eastern European or Scandinavian, as her surname might imply. But she is given no specific nationality, no context. Her family and relatives are far away, and remain vague. We soon cease asking ourselves practical questions as to why she is so strangely cast away in this Midland town and when she expects to leave or 'go home'. She is less a fully realised person than a carefully constructed rhetorical device through which Larkin can focus his ironies and poetic images.

Her foreignness may even seem at times part of a satire against Englishness, though Katherine is too indeterminate, nationally and culturally, to function as a reliable touchstone, and the hints do not develop into a coherent comedy of manners. Nevertheless there does seem to be a faintly comic irony in the way the familiar caricature elements of Englishness are presented through her responses. On their first meeting Robin remarks with a mechanically polite English self-deprecation: 'I hope you'll like English food . . . That again is supposed to be very bad – like the climate' (76). Katherine thinks of Robin 'first as dull, then as inarticulate . . . English boys were traditionally uncouth' (77). Jane sourly remarks that her brother is 'the perfect Englishman' (130) in his correct social manners. And Robin's 'barren perfection', the air of self-sufficiency which Katherine finds so intriguing, can be seen as a typically English reticence and ineptitude. There is an element of humourless farce in his gauche advance in the punt: 'He ducked his head and kissed her inexpertly with tight lips, as if dodging something that swept above their heads. It was not a bit like lovemaking, and she never thought of it as such till afterwards' (173).

Larkin's wan and unemphatic irony about Englishness here invites comparison with Amis's use of national stereotypes in *Lucky Jim*. Compared with Larkin, Amis has always been a man of cosmopolitan instincts, and incidentally, as he reveals in his *Memoirs*, early developed a taste for French food. In *Lucky Jim* however he evokes the familiar English xenophobia about eating habits to delightful comic effect. Dixon is highly gratified to hear of Michel Welch's illness, brought on (Dixon absurdly believes) by his pretentious liking for foreign food: 'spaghetti and dishes cooked in olive oil'. Dixon reflects: 'This seemed fit punishment for one so devoted to coagulated flour-and-water and peasants' butter-substitute, washed down, no doubt, by "real" black coffee of high viscosity' (Ch. 18). The phrases form a familiar cartoon stereotype, and make for vivid, if simple comedy. Paradoxically, Larkin, who outside his novels and poems proclaims an ardent xenophobia, shuddering with horror at the idea of marrying a foreigner (Jean Hartley, 96), absolutely refuses in his art to use the motif of foreignness in such a simply kinetic way. With extraordinary technical precision he contrives that foreignness in *A Girl in Winter* cannot possibly elicit the usual vulgar or picturesque response. With Katherine as his centre of consciousness the English characters are themselves foreign. She is foreign in England, but England is foreign to her. Foreignness acts as an agent of poetic detachment and stasis. This is a most surprising effect to have been conceived by any English writer, and points to the profound difference between Larkin the man and Larkin the artist.

But Katherine is not only foreign, she is also a woman. Part of her poetic quality derives from the author's sense of her otherness as a female. There is a distinctly female cast to her physical and emotional responses:

> They stood for a second on the top of the steps, the cold rising up their skirts, and began to walk down as a clock struck ten-fifteen . . . Katherine looked disproportionately strong and dark beside Miss Green, (26–7)

> Oh, but he was hopelessly muddled in her mind, for as he gave a bound up the steps towards her, his delicate, wary face struck again deeply in her, and his dark half-tousled head carried itself with such simultaneous independence and attention – attention, what was more, to her – that she herself felt like a servant.
>
> 'Staying here, are we?' he said, beginning to screw his racquet into its press. Her heart sank. She did not want to talk trivialities with him. (101)

Most important to the poetic effect is the fact that her female consciousness encloses the action, unencumbered by any intervening fictionalised male psychology. In this novel no Kemp mediates between the author and his dream of femaleness. Katherine, replacing 'Jill Bradley', moves to the foreground, taking over the novel's centre of consciousness, and her lyrical worlds of winter and summer replace the awkward Willow Gables fantasy. Through Katherine, as through 'Jill', Larkin participates in femaleness. She is the Other: feeling the cold rising up her skirts, toying with adolescent romantic yearnings, passively enduring Mr Anstey's and Robin's sexual harrassment.

Lik *Jill*, *A Girl in Winter* is a version of the Pygmalion myth, but a much more complex and poetically resonant one. On one level the second novel simply repeats the pattern of the first in a more direct form, as the male author brushes aside the uneasy authorial projection, Kemp, and fashions his dream-woman without mediation. At the end of the second novel, as in the first, the woman's sordid physical encounter with a man (Kemp, Robin) breaks the imaginative spell of the dream. Poetry is replaced by sex, and the beautiful statue is transformed from work of art to prosaic fellow human being. But in two important respects the second novel is more complex than the first. In the first place it includes a second rival Pygmalion figure. The myth is repeated *within* the story with the gender roles reversed. Within the story Katherine acts as the creative Pygmalion rather than the created statue. Robin Fennel and the summer idyll are her work of art (her 'Jill Bradley' and Willow Gables fantasy). She is no longer merely the object of male creative fantasy; she has become a subject in her own right, creating her own artistic object. At the climax of this novel Katherine does not simply, like 'Jill', lose her magic for her creator, as romantic male myth collides with reality. She suffers her own disillusion. Robin, the vehicle of her female myth, loses his magic for her, and also, significantly, for the author. To the end the reader shares her perceptions, remaining within her female consciousness, as she seeks to fend off disillusion through pure, negative images of cold and ice.

The second important new complexity is the author's dissociation of himself from the sordid masculine act which shatters her illusions. The final scene of the second novel reverses the emotional pattern of the first. *Jill* invites us to share Kemp's shame as he disgraces himself before Gillian; *A Girl in Winter* invites us to share Katherine's despair as she hopelessly submits to Robin's advances. The reader of the first novel participates in Kemp's drunken disgrace as he attempts to impose his pathetically unreal fantasy on a real schoolgirl. In the second novel, in contrast, the reader participates in the girl's distaste for a drunken man's crude destruction of the warm dream which insulated her from winter. Larkin has sealed his poetic empathy with the female consciousness far more effectively than in the first novel, but in doing so he has dissociated himself from the more prosaic and physical relationship with the woman to which his male protagonists aspire. Indeed in becoming the 'successful' lover of Katherine Robin proves himself quite unworthy of her. Her creator, the author, remains worthy of her in his own eyes only through rejecting the sordidness which Robin forces upon her. There is an unnerving aesthetic conclusiveness about the negativity of this resolution. In more biographical terms it seems to betray an intense sexual guilt on Larkin's part, and it is easy to see ominous implications here for Larkin's engagement, entered upon three years after this novel was completed.

With *A Girl in Winter* Larkin was uneasily aware that he had reached an impasse in his development as a novelist. But he could see no solution. He explained the problem gloomily as one of 'ideas', or 'theme':

> *The Kingdom of Winter* is rather unimpressive compared with *Jill*. But when you read it you will see why – it is a deathly book and has for theme the relinquishing of live response to life. The central character, Katherine, picks up where John left off and carries the story out into the frozen wastes – the kingdom of winter, to be exact. (20.ix.45)

Indeed, a work whose beauty is essentially contained in descriptions of winter and summer landscapes, and whose only physical relationship is one of utter sterility, seems to offer little promise of a future novelistic career for its author. Months later, when he sent a copy of the published book to Sutton he expressed disappointment with his inability to give it any Lawrentian guts or earth:

> Looking at it dispassionately I somehow don't care for it. It is a pitiless book, and it uses human beings to express an idea, rather than to express the truth about themselves.

Lawrence did that I know, but he had far greater natural sympathy for (I won't say 'with') people and anyway his ideas were probably better than mine. If I write another book, I shall try to be 'humbler' regarding people. (24.ii.47)

But, however Larkin expressed it, the problem is still the same as that with *Jill*: his notion of the novel as 'diffused poem'. Just as Katherine is unable to reconcile her poetic inner world with sordid reality, so her creator's poetic approach to the novel will never lead him to Lawrentian 'life' or 'sympathy for people'. Nor was he prepared to take the route of Woolf and Stevie Smith, and abandon the paraphernalia of realistic character and social context in favour of a freer poetic form. Instead he persisted with ghostly versions of Amis caricatures, called Jack Stormalong or Robin Fennel or Mr Anstey, manipulated by an inertly overcomplicated plot. Since he could not learn this formal lesson, the only answer for him, though he was reluctant to admit it, was to abandon the novel form and to write 'undiffused' poems instead.

FROM NOVELIST TO POET

In 1982 Larkin was still regretting the failure of his novelistic ambitions: 'I wanted to "be a novelist",' he said sadly, 'in a way I never wanted to "be a poet" ' (*RW*, 63). In an earlier interview he elaborated further:

> But I could never write a third novel, though I must have spent about five years trying to. I felt a bit cheated. I'd had visions of myself writing 500 words a day for six months, shoving the result off to the printer and going to live on the Côte d'Azur, uninterrupted except for the correction of proofs. It didn't happen like that – very frustrating.
>
> I still think novels are much more interesting than poems – a novel is so spreading, it can be so fascinating and so difficult. I think they were just too hard for me. I've said somewhere that novels are about other people and poems are about yourself. I think that was the trouble, really. I didn't know enough about other people, I didn't like them enough. (*RW*, 49)

It is difficult to believe that the young author of *A Girl in Winter* really deluded himself into believing that he could live on the Côte d'Azur on the proceeds of his novel-writing – unless his third novel was to be startlingly different from his first two. He recollects in the Introduction to the 1976 American edition of *Jill* that his 'sole payment' for both *Jill* and *The North Ship* was a cup of tea, bought by his publisher 'in a tea shop near Victoria Station' (*RW*, 26). And though he did receive a small advance from Faber and Faber for *A Girl in Winter* it must be suspected that this Mediterranean ambition has no more substance than a joke fantasy elaborated between himself and Amis at the time.

The letters which Larkin wrote immediately following the completion of *A Girl in Winter* paint a different picture. Larkin put up a brave show of purposeful artistic development:

> Now I am thinking of a third book in which the central character will pick up where Katherine left off and develop *logically* back to life again. In other words, the north ship will come back instead of being bogged up there in a glacier. Then I shall have finished this particular branch of soul-history (my own, of course) and what will happen then I don't know. (20.ix.45)

The word 'logically' here has a hollow ring. If these novels are records of his own soul-history, it might be expected that any move 'back to life again' must come from developments in his own experience, rather than by abstract aesthetic 'logic'. Is he perhaps referring, in these cagily indirect terms, to his relationship with Ruth Bowman, which had begun by this time, but was not to develop into an official engagement for over two years? However this may be, Larkin seems not to have found it easy to gain an imaginative grip on his third novel: 'The furious creation of these last two years has spent itself', he remarks despondently (17.x.45).

Discussion of the third and fourth novels, fragments of which are now lodged in the Brynmor Jones Library at Hull (together with an incomplete play, also written during this period) must wait until they become available for study. The letters to Sutton mention only one novel, part of the action of which was to be set in an art school. Kingsley Amis has reported that the other (which he calls the 'third novel') was to be 'a serio-comic account of the gradual involvement of a rising young executive in the motor industry, Sam Wagstaff, with a working-class girl he knocks down in his car coming home from the factory' (1982, 28). Amis's summary of this book suggests certain familiar problems. If Larkin treated this story in a similar way to *Jill*, it may be surmised that familiar difficulties must have manifested themselves in even more acute forms. How, for instance, would he treat this 'working-class girl'? The incongruous image of a female Whitbread realised through the poetic sensibility of a Katherine comes to mind. Even more intriguing is the hint that this novel was to be a 'serio-comic' work. Certainly the humourlessness of Larkin's completed novels makes a startling contrast with the rich ironic humour of his letters at this time, and also of much of the mature poetry which followed. But any speculation is idle at this stage, and may prove to be very wide of the mark.

At the time he broke his engagement and left for Belfast, Larkin gave up both his novels (Amis 1982, 28). Once he had reluctantly resigned himself to being a mere poet his artistic development dashed forward like a hussar – as he had forecast it would. The theme of fragile dream versus hard reality remains constant, and several of the poems depict crude masculine intrusions on female innocence ('Deceptions', 'If, My Darling', 'Sunny Prestatyn'). But the provisional, dramatised voice of lyric poetry exempts the writer from the moral and social responsibilities of the Lawrentian novelist, and the artistic effect is less strained and anxious. His early struggles with the novel form however (and his association with Amis) do have important implications for his poetic career. A number of his mature poems focus on stereotype characters of the same novelistic order as Whitbread and Mr Anstey: Arnold, Mr Bleaney, Jake Balokowsky, Warlock-Williams. But in the poems these figures are freed from the requirements of plot and social realism, becoming dramatised and ironised expressions of the poet's attitudes. As a poet he feels no obligation to 'become the whole of boredom' or 'Dully put up with all the wrongs of Man'. As Larkin said: 'to put this in its simplest terms, if you tell a novelist "Life's not like that", he has to do something about it. The poet simply replies, "No, but I am" ' (*RW*, 95–6).

3

'The experience. The beauty'

LARKIN'S LYRIC POETRY

The young Larkin approached the task of finding his own poetic voice with a business-like deliberation. The letters he wrote in the early 1940s show the poet bringing to bear on his own techniques the most ruthless analytical criticism. He never mistakes imitation for his own voice, and selects his models with astute judgement. A clear hierarchy of preferences emerges. D. H. Lawrence is at the top, though this influence is more a matter of spirit than technique. In April 1941, the eighteen-year-old poet hesitantly congratulates himself that one of his imitations is 'Much nearer Lawrence than Auden' (16.iv.41). At this stage it is the early non-political Auden who is the most admired technical model, with Dylan Thomas and others some way behind. The poetic novice experiments with styles, deliberately indulging his 'fatal gift of pastiche' (he borrows the phrase from Isherwood), and readily conceding that most of his work is 'just like any other shit by Day Lewis or anyone else', though 'odd phrases', he adds, brightening for a second, are 'just like Auden' (16.iv.41). In August 1942 he tells Sutton briskly: 'I have ... changed my poetic style, writing pompous, windy effusions of the war in the style of Stephen Spender' (5.viii.42). Later the same month he laments: 'My poytry is all to buggery at present. The pure wine of Auden has been shamefully adulterated by Spender's still lemonade and Dylan's Welsh whiskey' (17.viii.42). Even after he has adopted the portentous tones of Yeats in his poems, he still exercises the same self-critical rigour, dismissing a piece with which he is pleased as 'Yeats mainly' (21.iv.44). A steady sureness of purpose is evident in the deliberate combination and recombination of literary influences which ιnarks Larkin's juvenilia, as he felt his way towards the moment when his own voice would emerge through the echoes of others.

In the retrospective Introduction to the 1966 reissue of *The North Ship* (1945), Larkin briskly summed up this early period:

> Looking back, I find in the poems not one abandoned self but several – the ex-schoolboy, for whom Auden was the only alternative to 'old-fashioned' poetry; the under-graduate, whose work a friend affably characterized as 'Dylan Thomas, but you've a sentimentality that's all your own'; and the immediately post-Oxford self, isolated in Shropshire with a complete Yeats stolen from the local girls' school. (*RW*, 28)

The impact of Yeats, who all but drowns out the other influences in *The North Ship*, was the result of an inspiring visit by the poet Vernon Watkins to the Oxford University English Club in 1943, after which, Larkin says, 'I spent the next three years trying to write like Yeats' (*RW*, 29). Nevertheless, despite its imitativeness, there is a seductively nerveless quality about much of *The North Ship* which is, in a minor way, distinctive and original. A poet who can write pastiche with such confident facility has already mastered some important elements of the poetic craft:

> To write one song, I said,
> As sad as the sad wind
> That walks around my bed,
> Having one simple fall
> As a candle-flame swells, and is thinned,
> As a curtain stirs by the wall
> – For this I must visit the dead.
>
> (*CP*, 291)

This is an undisguised transposition of Yeats's 'The Fisherman' into something more routinely 'poetic'. But none the less it has a surefooted gusto about it which disarms criticism, and could perhaps be considered rather in the light of a juvenile 'homage' to Yeats than a simple imitation. At times Larkin's poetic gestures in *The North Ship* seem not far from parody, and perhaps an element of half-conscious humour is detectable. The mannered poses are enjoyed with evident youthful enthusiasm:

> Love, we must part now: do not let it be
> Calamitous and bitter. In the past
> There has been too much moonlight and self-pity . . .
>
> (*CP*, 280)

But increasingly the authentic voice of Larkin himself makes itself heard through the bardic phrase-making. 'And the wave sings because it is moving', for instance, completed in 1946, shortly after the publication of *The North Ship*, is a fascinating blend of strained poeticism and assured eloquence. Every phrase shows a process of self-conscious technical adjustment, as the poet's craftsmanship struggles to impose itself on essentially second-hand material:

> Death is a cloud alone in the sky with the sun.
> Our hearts, turning like fish in the green wave,
> Grow quiet in its shadow. For in the word death
> There is nothing to grasp; nothing to catch or claim;
> Nothing to adapt the skill of the heart to, skill
> In surviving, for death it cannot survive,
> Only resign the irrecoverable keys.
>
> (*CP*, 6)

The simple, even stark choice of syntax in 'Death is a cloud alone in the sky with the sun', together with the grammatically patterned anapaestic phrases ('in the sky with the sun') make the line eloquent and memorable in a way which already anticipates Larkin's mature style. But the image is still not distinctive enough, and the gesture is romantically mannered. The image of 'Our hearts, turning like fish in the green wave', on the other hand, is more arresting, and its treatment shows Larkin's characteristically unobtrusive craftsmanship. The reversal of the iambic metre in the second foot ('turning') mimics the twist of the fish, while both the stresses of the last two feet are thrown into the final sensuous phrase ('green wave'). The next lines strike an authentic Larkinesque note of elegiac resignation: 'For in the word death/ There is nothing to grasp; nothing to catch or claim.' But the effect is rather spoiled by the tone of Yeatsian grandiloquence. Moreover there are too many verbs of similar meaning ('grasp', 'catch', 'claim'), and the alliteration of 'catch' and 'claim' consequently sounds lame. On the other hand the next phrase, 'Nothing to adapt the skill of the heart to', rings true. Its naturally faltering rhythm, with its hanging preposition ('to'), stumbles against the metre, giving a touching pathos to the human defencelessness which the poet is evoking. Such delicately contrived interactions of metre and rhythm lie at the heart of Larkin's mature achievement: 'Writing poetry', he said in 1982, 'is playing off the natural rhythms and word-order of speech against the artificialities of rhyme and metre' (*RW*, 71). Even the brassily portentous phrase-making of 'the irrecoverable keys' of life is partly redeemed by the stammering immediacy of 'irrecoverable'.

In an essay of 1968 Larkin attributed the growing assurance of his style in the years following *The North Ship* to a chance reading of Thomas Hardy, which cured him of his Yeatsian pretensions, and enabled him at last to speak with his own voice. In January 1946 he moved to new 'digs' in Wellington which faced East, and found himself being woken by the sun at about six every morning:

> so I used to read, and it happened that I had Hardy's own selection of his poems, and I began to read them and was immediately struck by them . . . When I came to Hardy it was with the sense of relief that I didn't have to try and jack myself up to a concept of poetry that lay outside my own life – this is perhaps what I felt Yeats was trying to make me do. One could simply relapse back into one's own life and write from it. (*RW*, 175)

The example of Yeats had imposed on the young Larkin a mythic rhetoric which was untrue to his sensibility. In contrast, Hardy pointed the way to a more personal, less broadly histrionic approach. 'He's not a transcendental writer, he's not a Yeats, he's not an Eliot' (*RW*, 175). Hardy's example relieved Larkin of the burden of having to embody some Yeatsian myth of 'The Poet', or to adopt a public role. He need no longer pretend to speak from a bardic height to the audience below.

There is an intimate violence in Larkin's later attacks on the Irish poet, perhaps not unmixed with a certain envy of what he saw as Yeats's smug rhetorical egotism. In 1974 he is reported as having referred (in private) to 'That shit Yeats, farting out his histrionic rubbish!' (Watt, 175). Larkin's notorious *Oxford Book of Twentieth Century English Verse*, published in 1973, subtly denies the stature of Yeats, and constructs a self-consciously 'conservative' canon, running from Hardy, through Kipling and Housman to Betjeman, glued together with second-rate imitations of Hardy. The story told by Larkin's own poetry, however, is a different one. As Edna Longley has remarked: 'more of Yeats . . . survives in Larkin's poetry than he would have us believe. – Can a writer ever totally obliterate the memory of his first literary love?' (Longley, 64). Larkin had early steeped himself in Yeats' poetry and it was from Yeats (and to a lesser extent Auden), rather than from Hardy, that he learnt the music of his phrasing. This was a permanent and indelible lesson, whose impact can still be detected in Larkin's verse long after any audible echo of the Irish poet has faded. Phrases like 'the million-petalled flower/ Of being here', or 'nothing contravenes/ The coming dark', or 'That vast moth-eaten musical brocade/ Created to pretend we never die' do not echo Yeats in any specific way, but their unabashed poetic elevation and their sophisticated control of tone ultimately derive from Yeats's example. Also Larkin's self-conscious manipulation of large abstract poetic symbols, the sea-scape in 'Absences', 'high windows', the moon in 'Sad Steps', is quite unlike anything in Hardy. Like Yeats and unlike Hardy, Larkin is thoroughly 'literary' in his instincts. His work resonates with recollections and half-echoes of previous literature, and with familiar cultural references. Though he learns an intimate quietness of tone from Hardy, he never approaches the homespun unliterariness of Hardy's most distinctive poems.

The influence of Hardy is seen in the muted plainness of some of Larkin's phrases, and above all in the commonplace, everyday situations of many of his mature poems: the old music sheets of 'Love Songs in Age', the domestic scene of 'Reference Back', the church monument in 'An Arundel Tomb'. Essentially Hardy's impact on Larkin took the form of a revelation of principle: 'One could simply relapse back into one's own life and write from it.' 'Hardy taught one to feel, rather than to write', Larkin says; 'of course one has to use one's own language and one's own jargon and one's own situations' (*RW*, 175-6). By the time he came to Hardy, Larkin had already matured beyond the need to imitate any other poet, so he rarely echoes Hardy's style as he had earlier copied and absorbed Yeats's. Moreover Larkin's aesthetic attitudes remain, throughout his life, 'Yeatsian' in some essential respects. Larkin's rejection of the Irish poet's mythifying left him, not with rustic Hardyesque pessimism, nor with the unassuming poetry of 'the common man', but with a pure, intense aestheticism, peculiar to himself, which remained his nearest approach to an artistic 'philosophy'. At the end of his poetic career in 1982, he was questioned about his conservative-sounding view that poetry grows out of a desire to 'preserve'. What was it, he was asked, that he was attempting to 'preserve'. His answer was one which Yeats might have given at the turn of the century: 'the experience. The beauty' (*RW*, 68). As Andrew Motion has said, Larkin's mature work is best seen not as a rejection of Yeats in favour of Hardy, but as an unresolved dialectic between the two influences which generates something quite new and original (Motion, 82).

Turning from Larkin's precursors to his contemporaries, we find a more confusing picture. In the 1950s, when his work first came to notice, its unique originality could scarcely have been recognised. Consequently a great deal of early criticism of his work now seems to be preoccupied with transient inessentials, particularly the attempt to identify his work with current literary and social fashions. There seems today, for instance, more historical than literary interest in tracing Larkin's position within the so-called 'Movement'. The pessimistic tone of *The Less Deceived*, together with Larkin's contempt for the 'mad lads' of Modernism, encouraged among literary journalists the idea that he belonged to a loose group of post-war poets and novelists, who had been described in a *Spectator* article of 1954 as:

> bored by the despair of the Forties, not much interested in suffering, and extremely impatient of poetic sensibility, especially poetic sensibility about 'the writer and society' . . . The Movement, as well as being anti-phoney, is anti-wet; sceptical, robust, ironic . . . (in Morrison, 2)

Some of Larkin's poetry indeed shows some of these elements, but they do not constitute a programme shared on any significant level with his contemporaries. As Blake Morrison shows in his account of the literary history of the 1950s, the writers who were identified as belonging to 'The Movement', Larkin, Kingsley Amis, Donald Davie, D. J. Enright, Thom Gunn, John Wain and Elizabeth Jennings, share a common 1950s 'feel', but little else. They belong together historically, but on the literary level they differ immensely. As Larkin himself said: 'it certainly never occurred to me that I had anything in common with Thom Gunn, or Donald Davie, for instance, or they with each other' (in Hamilton, 72). Most importantly, as Morrison's analyses demonstrate, there is an embarrassing gulf in literary complexity between Larkin and all the others. Though parallels can be drawn between Larkin's poetry and that of Amis or Enright, of more essential literary interest today, now that the stature of Larkin's work is recognised, are parallels with other major writers from different historical periods.

Even more misleading, because so vigorously promoted by Larkin himself in his later years, is the parallel with the older poet Betjeman. Only in one sense is Larkin's poetry essentially like Betjeman's. They share a bleak elegiac reflectiveness which expresses itself in terms of what Larkin calls 'the furniture of our lives' (*RW*, 211). Thus Betjeman's 'On a Portrait of a Deaf Man' movingly recalls his dead father's domestic habits: his painting in oils, his liking for 'Potatoes in their skin' and 'the rain-washed Cornish air'. Similarly Larkin in 'An April Sunday brings the snow' is movingly reminded of his father by the jam which he made before his death. Apart from this basic similarity however these poems could scarcely be more different. Betjeman's poem aims at instantaneous effects. Its metre is unvarying and swift; its imagery surrealistic and melodramatic, structured upon bold contrasts between the homely image of his live father and macabre images of his body's decay:

> He would have liked to say good-bye,
>   Shake hands with many friends,
> In Highgate now his finger-bones
>   Stick through his finger-ends.
>
> (Betjeman, 97)

The effect is garish, an unsettling combination of humour and grief. Larkin's metre and imagery, in contrast, do not advertise their presence so loudly, nor are we given a characterful sketch of the dead man. The poem focuses singlemindedly on the poet's meditative thoughts as he stores the jam away in the kitchen. This central image gathers resonance until the poet's grief quietly overflows:

> Behind the glass, under the cellophane,
> Remains your final summer – sweet
> And meaningless, and not to come again.
>
> (CP, 21)

Larkin's work presents itself as a private matter of his own feelings. Its 'universality' is achieved by persuading the reader to share those feelings. Betjeman's thoughts, on the other hand, turn explicitly to the claims to objective 'universality' of the Church. His poem ends with a public theological challenge:

> You, God, who treat him thus and thus,
> Say 'Save his soul and pray.'
> You ask me to believe You and
> I only see decay.
>
> (Betjeman, 97)

Significantly Larkin chose to include in *The Oxford Book* not this histrionic poem, but Betjeman's more relaxed and novelistic, if less poetically intense, reminiscence of his father in *Summoned by Bells* (*OBTCEV*, 382–5).

A similar contrast between the two poets emerges from a comparison between Betjeman's 'The Metropolitan Railway', whose 'poignantly brutal' effect Larkin so admired (*RW*, 211), and apparently similar poems by the younger poet. Betjeman's poem presents an image of a newly-wed Edwardian couple, travelling to their suburban home, and then, with edgy half-rhyme, contrasts their present state:

> Cancer has killed him. Heart is killing her.
> The trees are down. An Odeon flashes fire
> Where stood their villa by the murmuring fir.
>
> (Betjeman, 213)

In its stark juxtaposition of the beginning and end of a marriage through the linking image of the repeated railway journey this piece seems not dissimilar to several poems by Larkin, for instance 'Love Songs in Age', where the rediscovered music sheets similarly reflect the passage of time. There is also a parallel with other poems by Larkin such as 'I Remember, I Remember', which focus on scenes viewed from a train. One critic has already compared Betjeman's poem with 'The Whitsun Weddings' (Hassan, 90–3). Again however there is a profound difference between the two poets. Betjeman is interested in the 'furniture of our lives' for its own sake. He has a real affection for the Metropolitan Railway as a social institution, and this poem is as much a celebration of the décor and atmosphere of Baker Street station buffet as it is an elegy for this particular suburban couple:

> Early Electric! Sit you down and see,
> 'Mid this fine woodwork and a smell of dinner,
> A stained-glass windmill and a pot of tea,
> And sepia views of leafy lanes in PINNER . . .
>
> (Betjeman, 212)

Larkin's attention in 'Love Songs in Age', by contrast, is single-mindedly concentrated on the woman, as she contemplates her lost, irrecoverable youth. The reader is placed within her consciousness, and the song-sheets are an intense vehicle of emotion rather than a subject of celebration or picturesque interest in their own right. This is a consistent difference between the two poets. The familiar domestic 'furniture' of life upon which Larkin's poems focus (an empty church, blossom on plum-trees, 'That vase') never becomes part of a coherent, culturally specific myth, as does Betjeman's (suburban villas, Odeons, 'Rovers and Austins', Westminster Abbey). It is true that in 'Reference Back' and 'For Sidney Bechet' Larkin focuses on his own personal enthusiasm for jazz, which was as intense as that of Betjeman for Victorian and Edwardian architecture. But the success of Larkin's poems does not depend in the slightest on the reader's complicity in his enthusiasm.

It is popularly assumed that the two poets share a sense of place and a common Englishness. This is quite wrong. Betjeman celebrates the communal solidarity of the British middle classes, high and low, glorying in the easily recognisable 'Englishness' of car brandnames, places and lifestyles, as in the extract from 'Beside the Seaside' which Larkin includes in *The Oxford Book*:

> Solihull, Headingley and Golders Green,
> Preston and Swindon, Manchester and Leeds,

Braintree and Bocking, hear the sea! the sea!
The smack of breakers upon windy rocks,
Spray blowing backwards from their curling walls
Of green translucent water. England leaves
Her centre for her tide-line.

(*OBTCEV*, 372)

Larkin would not have so confidently appropriated the word 'England' to his own imaginative province. 'England' as a geographical and political abstraction does not feature in his poems, and Larkin's poetic landscape scarcely ever serves as a focus for collective social euphoria, as Betjeman's does. With the partial exception of such late exercises as 'Going, Going' (*CP*, 189), and 'Bridge for the Living' (*CP*, 203), both of which significantly were commissioned works, and perhaps also the mutedly Betjemanesque 'Show Saturday' (*CP*, 199), Larkin's landscapes are personal and specific rather than public, a matter of his own contingent association with particular places: Oxford, London, Coventry, Hull. The historical, mythic 'Oxford' of literary tradition, for instance, forms a strange transfigured undercurrent in *Jill*, but is quite absent elsewhere in his work. Oxford appears once only, merely as the city where he and Monica Jones failed to meet each other. And this poem's ironic title, 'Poem about Oxford' (*CP*, 179), is in itself a mock-heroic comment on the Oxford of literary legend. Betjeman's poems about Oxford, on the other hand, 'Myfanwy at Oxford', 'St. Barnabas, Oxford' and 'May-Day Song for North Oxford', are a nostalgic medley of student rituals and historical echoes: 'Cherwell mist', cycle rides to Boar's Hill, and loving appreciations of church architecture.

Larkin's landscapes are less picturesque and less simply euphoric than those of Betjeman. Though one critic detects in 'MCMXIV' a 'somewhat Betjemanesque . . . conservative Larkin' (Whalen, 41), its images are in fact subject to an ironic placing quite alien to the older poet's glowing vision of Victorian and Edwardian England. The central motif of the poem is a familiar focus of nostalgia: a group of young men enlisting for the Great War, seen as in a faded photograph. But the poet shows himself quite aware of the mediated quality of this image. Larkin is not naïvely expressing 'nostalgia for a pre-First World War England [he] never experienced' (Osborne 183). Rather he is dramatising a particularly potent cultural myth of the later twentieth century, with all its complex ironies. The archaic elements in the scene, for instance – the date in roman numerals, 'farthings and sovereigns', 'tin advertisements', 'differently-dressed servants', 'the pubs/ Wide open all day' (*CP*, 127) – are listed in a tone of elegiac pensiveness rather than rhetorical enthusiasm. Nor does the poet conservatively celebrate the pre-war social order: the servants have 'tiny rooms in huge houses', and the 'innocence' of the grinning young men, queuing up to die in the trenches 'as if it were all /An August Bank Holiday lark', is heavily ironic. The phrase 'fields/ Shadowing Domesday lines', with its evocation of dim historical vistas, may seem to show the 'deeply patriotic . . . feeling for his native country' with which Larkin is frequently credited (Draper, 95). On the other hand there is nothing particularly patriotic about lamenting the unprecedented slaughter of the Great War which, the poem asserts, broke for ever the historical continuity implied by this phrase.

These complexities of tone show that the poet is not concerned simply to affirm a familiar shared myth of England, whether mediaeval or Edwardian-Georgian. His real subject is the fragile human idealism which these myths embody. There is a faint, but profound irony in the quiet, hyperbolic repetition of 'Never such innocence,/ Never before or since' – not a satirical or destructive irony, but an indication that the words are more the assertion of an emotional attitude than a statement of historical fact:

> Never such innocence,
> Never before or since,
> As changed itself to past
> Without a word – the men
> Leaving the gardens tidy,
> The thousands of marriages
> Lasting a little while longer:
> Never such innocence again.
> (*CP*, 127–8)

The absence of a main verb ('As changed itself', rather than 'Has changed itself') also serves to show that the poet is not simply describing the impact of a particular, unique event. He is giving expression to one of those irresistible myths of innocence and beauty through which, in all ages, we seek to come to terms with the suffering and transience of the world. The pathos is intensified by the sudden ahistorical plainness of the language in this last stanza, which abruptly strips away the ideological rhetoric, reducing a rich, consolatory image of a lost Golden Age to the painfully simple and vulnerable reality of marriages and tidy gardens.

Larkin's poetic imagination finds no security in patriotism, nor in celebrating his national or class identity. He remains at an ironic distance from such ingenuous commitments. He does not define himself as Waugh and Betjeman do, through a network of establishment rituals: tennis, church on Sunday, subalterns and debutantes, Henley Regatta. He does not express his tribal identity like Betjeman by 'going up to town'. His journey to London in 'The Whitsun Weddings' is both more thoroughly provincial than anything in Betjeman and more universal. Larkin himself seems half-aware of the difference when he remarks on the way Betjeman's poetry answers so neatly to T. S. Eliot's definition of Englishness in *Notes Towards the Definition of Culture*:

> And what is this 'whole way of life' that a poet should (presumably) concern himself with expressing? Eliot was obliging enough to leave us a list of its properties: 'Derby Day, Henley Regatta, Cowes, the twelfth of August, a cup final, the dog races, the pin table, the dart board, Wensleydale cheese, boiled cabbage cut in sections, beetroot in vinegar, nineteenth-century gothic churches, and the music of Elgar.'
>
> Now if this passage reminds us of anyone's poetry, it is Betjeman's rather than Eliot's or anyone else's. (*RW*, 218).

There is a hint of irritated sarcasm here – '(presumably)', 'obliging enough', 'properties' – as though Larkin had recognised in Eliot's American snapshot of 'Englishness' the perspective of a tourist, well briefed by the guidebook in what to look out for. Certainly none of the institutions or rituals which Eliot mentions has any place in Larkin's own work, except as ironically placed stereotype.

It is not in Larkin's poetry that we should seek the sources of his liking for the older poet. The comments he makes about Betjeman in reviews, and also the choice of Betjeman's poems in *The Oxford Book of Twentieth Century English Verse*, point to a simpler, less imaginatively interesting reason for his championing of Betjeman. For a writer so ideologically insecure as Larkin Betjeman seems to have triggered a release of inhibitions. The middle-class librarian found in the upper-middle-class man of leisure, and best-selling poet, a champion of literary and political conservatism to whose side he could rally. His expressions of literary allegiance to the older poet are crude in the extreme: 'I may flatter myself, but I think in one sense I'm like Evelyn Waugh or John Betjeman, in that there's not much to *say* about my work' (*RW*, 53–4). There is a shallow pugnacity in his assertions of Betjeman's importance: 'Can it be that, as Eliot dominated the first half of the twentieth century, the second half will derive from Betjeman? I do not think this is as completely unlikely a suggestion as it might first appear' (*RW*, 218). Larkin's evaluation of Betjeman's poetry shows an indulgent attitude towards crude and explicit versifying which he would never have permitted in his own work. He quotes, for instance, a poem in which Betjeman (whose inherited money enabled him to pursue his aesthetic enthusiasms at leisure) attacks the factory-worker's forty-hour week:

> An eight-hour day for all, and more than three
> Of these are occupied with making tea
> And talking over what we all agree –
> Though 'Music while you work' is now our wont,
> It's not so nice as 'Music while you don't'.

Larkin comments preposterously:

> most literary critics these days are on the left wing, and so are unlikely to be appreciative of a passage such as the one above. For my part, I find the last five lines not only a pertinent summary of a subject no other present-day British poet has tried to deal with, but singularly unforgettable.
>
> (*RW*, 213)

A faintly hectic note of provocation is audible in the overemphatic phrases of the last sentence. It is of course not only 'left-wing' critics who will find Betjeman's doggerel crude in sentiment and rhythmically banal. Significantly, in his review of Betjeman's *Collected Poems* in *Listen*, which he chose not to reprint in *Required Writing*, Larkin adopted a somewhat more complex tone. There he makes an awkward attempt to answer the critics' attacks on 'what they call [Betjeman's] readiness to side with the richer governing class in order to laugh at those with different class habits' (*Listen* 3, Spring

1959, 19), by pointing to the light, unsatirical quality of Betjeman's working-class stereotypes. He also hints at a quite sober assessment of Betjeman's poetic limitations, referring to the 'primitive vivacity' by which Betjeman 'captures the reader's attention without his intellectual consent' (15).

Their class and politics may have drawn Larkin and Betjeman together, but their poetry is poles apart. Though they both employ social stereotypes, for instance, their attitude to them is very different. Despite apparent similarities, Betjeman's 'Fair Elaine the bobby-soxer,/ Fresh-complexioned with Innoxa', his comic lower-class policeman in 'The Arrest of Oscar Wilde at the Cadogan Hotel' ('Mr Woilde, we 'ave come for tew take yew/ Where felons and criminals dwell'), belong to a simpler, less problematic world than the 'unspeakable wives/ . . . skinny as whippets' in 'Toads', the newly-weds in 'The Whitsun Weddings' or the 'girls with hair-dos' in 'The Building'. Similarly the technical achievement of their poetry is very different. While many works by Betjeman are immediately recognisable by their attractive anapaestic gusto or iambic doggerel, and by their pungently distinctive imagery, the 'Larkinesque' is a more subtle and complex matter of tones and nuances, not so easily reducible to mere metrical preference or 'characteristic' images. Christopher Ricks expresses something of the absurdity of Larkin's respectful admiration for Betjeman's minor talent in a comment made in 1965: 'His favourite living poet is that twangingly nostalgic relict, John Betjeman, whose *Collected Poems* Larkin went so far as [to] review twice. (Betjeman reviewed *The Whitsun Weddings* only once)' (Ricks, 6).

VERBAL DEVICES

The key to the understanding of Larkin's poetry lies here, in his refusal to adopt a consistent self-defining personal myth, such as those of Yeats or Betjeman, or an ideological programme such as that supposedly adopted by 'The Movement'. His numerous imaginative self-projections, as insouciant bachelor, as comic failure with women, as 'indigestible sterility' create a network of ironies rather than a secure identity. His refusal to define himself in such terms could be seen negatively as an aspect of his 'fundamentally passive attitude to poetry (and life too, I suppose)' (in George Hartley 1982,

88). He remains true to the diversity of his experience: he does not strain to impose a consistent pattern upon it. Thomas Hardy taught him that one could 'simply relapse back into one's own life' and still be a poet: 'He's not a transcendental writer, he's not a Yeats, he's not an Eliot' (*RW*, 175). But this denial of transcendence is also a refusal to take imaginative short-cuts. It is the distinctive strength of Larkin's poetry stubbornly to resist demystification in terms of anything more abstract than 'the experience' or 'the experience. The beauty' (*RW*, 68). His poetry is distrustful of its own ulterior motives in a way which the more egotistical works of Yeats and Eliot are not. 'I've never been didactic, never tried to make poetry *do* things, never gone out to look for it. I waited for it to come to me, in whatever shape it chose' (*RW*, 74). His work may lack some kinds of pretension; but it also entirely lacks pretentiousness.

Larkin's determination to avoid didacticism, to remain attentive, waiting for it to come, produces the peculiar mixture of extreme aestheticism and bald practicality which marks his few uneasy attempts to define the nature of his creativity. In the terse 'Statement' which he sent to D. J. Enright in 1955 he said:

> I write poems to preserve things I have seen/thought/felt (if I may so indicate a composite and complex experience) both for myself and for others, though I feel that my prime responsibility is to the experience itself, which I am trying to keep from oblivion for its own sake. Why I should do this I have no idea, but I think the impulse to preserve lies at the bottom of all art. (*RW*, 79)

When he restated his position in 1964, he described the preservation process in more practical terms: 'Some years ago I came to the conclusion that to write a poem was to construct a verbal device that would preserve an experience indefinitely by reproducing it in whoever read the poem.' This sounds more like a technical manual than an aesthetic programme. And Larkin goes on to imply that this minimal 'theory' was of value less in itself than as a practical aid to composition ('As a working definition, this satisfied me sufficiently to enable individual poems to be written'), and goes on to joke about 'verbal pickling' (*RW*, 83). His comments on his own art are concerned less to analyse the sources of his inspiration than to fend off analysis. 'I've never had "ideas" about poetry' (*RW*, 76) he said with a shudder of distaste, as at some desecration, 'To me it's always been a personal, almost physical release or solution to a complex pressure of needs – wanting to create, to justify, to praise, to explain, to externalize, depending on the circumstances' (*RW*, 76). And his satirical mimicking of the glib Freudianisms of 'Jake Balokowsky' in 'Posterity' (*CP*, 170) evidences his distaste for (even fear of) attempts to 'explain away' his creative processes.

The great strength of this attitude towards poetry is its fundamental authenticity, and the flexibility which it gives to the poet's rhetoric. Larkin has no programme to fulfil, no Byzantium to seek out, no 'still point of the turning world' to which all his experience must be related. Set loose from such anchorage his imagination can be responsive to every different, contradictory twist of his experience, every new insight, however unprecedented. None of his poems is made to fit a prepared context of meaning. Each one is forced to justify itself imaginatively on its own terms: 'As a guiding principle I believe that every poem must be its own sole freshly created universe' (*RW*, 79). The poems which bear this out most clearly are perhaps those mood-pieces which evoke irreducible, half-conscious states of being, or responses to environment and season. The subjects of 'Coming', 'The Importance of Elsewhere', 'As Bad as a Mile', 'A slight relax of air where cold was', 'The Card-Players', are instantly recognisable and familiar, but quite unexpected and original. If we set out to trace one of Larkin's more explicit 'themes' through his work, say death, or love, or marriage, we find a range of different, often contradictory positions and attitudes. The reader might be tempted for instance, on the strength of such first-person poems of the 1950s as 'To My Wife', 'Reasons for Attendance' and 'Self's the Man', to simplify Larkin's work in terms of a personal myth of selfish bachelordom. But no such consistent programme governs his work. These poems themselves are rich in ironic undertones, and moreover represent only one of Larkin's modes of treating the topic. Not only does the earlier 'Wedding-Wind', spoken in the person of a newly-married woman, belong to a different imaginative universe from these works, so also do such other poems of the 1950s as 'Long roots moor summer to our side of earth', congratulating a woman on her wedding, 'Maiden Name', delicately sharing a married woman's sense of approaching age, 'Love Songs in Age', looking back from widowhood to early romance, and 'The Whitsun Weddings', in which marriage becomes a general unifying assertion of common humanity.

One source of the diversity of Larkin's poems is the range of viewpoint which his works adopt. Some poems sound like personal responses to his immediate situation, while others are presented in the form of detached third-person reflections. In his 'Statement' of 1955 Larkin says: 'Generally my poems are related . . . to my own personal life, but by no means always, since I can imagine horses I have never seen or the emotions of a bride without ever having been a woman or married' (*RW*, 79). Indeed Larkin's poems empathising with married women or animals are often more intimately personal, in their indirect implications, than those in the bold first person. And the poems which do present themselves as first person comments on 'my own personal life' take no consistent position, covering the widest spectrum from the insouciant 'Self's the Man' to the pensive 'Reference Back' and the anguished 'Love Again'. Kingsley Amis has aptly called Larkin a 'poet of sensation' (1982, 30). He possesses to an extreme degree the lyric poet's ability to capture life as process, without striving to pin it down or harmonise it into an abstract philosophy – beyond the truisms that youth is sweet, love fades, and death awaits us. All Larkin's work is fundamentally autobiographical; but not in the sense of a worked out verdict on life in general, nor an 'apology' for his own life. Rather it embodies, 'preserves' experiences for their own sake.

Two early poems, 'At Grass' and 'Wires', both concerned with domestic animals in a field, and both in the detached third person, may be compared to illustrate Larkin's characteristic imaginative processes. 'At Grass', completed in January 1950, is one of Larkin's most profound works. It was a favourite with its author, who allowed his drafts of the poem to be published, in order to give readers an insight into the process of its composition (*Phoenix*, 1973/4, 91–103). It also offers a test-case for the ideological reading of Larkin, since, as in the case of 'MCMXIV', some critics have detected in it a subtext of conservative nostalgia. Like many of Larkin's most complex works its opening is undramatic, neutrally descriptive in tone. The poet seems unwilling to force meanings on the scene; rather he attentively waits for them to develop:

> The eye can hardly pick them out
> From the cold shade they shelter in,
> Till wind distresses tail and mane;
> Then one crops grass, and moves about

79

> \- The other seeming to look on –
> And stands anonymous again.
>
> (*CP*, 29)

By this point the reader is already troubled by the implications with which the poet's responses are charged. The ominous 'cold shade' in which the horses are 'sheltering' clearly carries undertones of death. The phrase is a heavy spondee, and sounds curiously formal; the reader may be reminded of the archaic poetic locution 'the shades'. It seems that this is to be a familiar elegy, expressing through the image of the retired horses our general apprehension of death. But the horses are also quite naturally evoked, as horses. The 'sh' alliteration ('shade . . . shelter') serves to emphasise the verb, creating an unexplained uneasiness. The horses are apparently 'sheltering' from warmth and light. The contradiction beautifully catches the irrational nervousness of the uncomprehending animals, shy of any exposure, not knowing what to fear. The sense of threat is reinforced by the rather poetic-sounding word 'distresses', which seems to transfer itself from the mere physical effect of the wind on mane to the emotions of the animals. Simply as an evocation of the demeanour of highly-strung racehorses these lines are already masterly.

But this atmospheric description also serves to embody the emotional tensions of the poet, whose function in this poem is somewhat more than that of a detached elegist. The first line has casually referred to the physical distance between the viewer and the horses. There is poignancy in the fact that the speaker can barely see them as they merge into the background. They are effaced, physically fading into indistinctness as their fame recedes and death approaches. And this is not merely a physical distance. The author doubts that these horses, dumb animals that they are, have any comprehension of their role in his human world: '– The other *seeming* to look on –': 'seeming', only, in a parody of the race spectators of previous days. It is not only the eye which can hardly 'pick them out', it is also the mind.

In the next lines the poet still strains to make the horses out, but now across time rather than space:

> Yet fifteen years ago, perhaps
> Two dozen distances sufficed

> To fable them . . .

The brilliant choice of the verbs, 'sufficed' and 'fable', makes it possible for the poet to summarise the horses' racing careers in the beautifully elliptical noun phrase 'Two dozen distances'. The insubstantial abstraction is strangely telling, its technical racing signific’ation (as in 'over the distance') acting as a literal focus for the other more resonant connotations of 'distance' which have haunted the poem from the beginning. 'Distances' would be no unsuitable alternative title for the poem. The poet is at a distance from the horses, physically and metaphysically; and the horses are at a distance from their former racing careers, in time, and also existentially. They have never really participated in the human world, which remains bewilderingly alien to them, with its competitiveness ('Cups and Stakes and Handicaps'), fashions ('parasols'), and wars (hinted at in 'Squadrons of empty cars'). The horses, 'anonymous again', have now returned to their own animal world, having slipped the names which the human society they never understood gave them for its own purposes.

The fourth stanza returns to the darkening field:

> Do memories plague their ears like flies?
> They shake their heads. Dusk brims the shadows.
> Summer by summer all stole away,
> The starting-gates, the crowds and cries –
> All but the unmolesting meadows.

The feebleness of the poet's wit in detecting in the shaking heads a human gesture of negation only serves to heighten the reader's awareness that such gestures are meaningless to the horses themselves. (Earlier drafts have the more obviously pathetic anthropomorphism 'They hang their heads'.) As the dark thickens, the poetic texture becomes denser, with too much stress and too many syllables for the metre ('Dusk brims the shadows'), the extra, hypermetrical syllable in 'shadows' giving the line a dying fall. Then follow a couple of lines of familiar poetic diction suddenly focused into a most surprising phrase, 'unmolesting meadows'. After an uncomprehending life of harassment by human beings, the horses can fall back on their instinctual certainty that grass, at least, is safe. Taken out o context this phrase would seem to be preposterously unworkable; who expects meadows to 'molest' anything? In its place it is haunting and immediately memorable. Unique to this context, it has no conceivable meaning outside it. The original form of the phrase in the worksheets, 'unmeasured meadows' (in antithesis to their racetrack careers, 'measured' in money), is in comparison feebly euphonious and didactic (*Phoenix*, 1973/4, 100).

The climax of 'At Grass' is a verbal device of the subtlest intricacy:

> Almanacked, their names live; they
>
> Have slipped their names, and stand at ease,
> Or gallop for what must be joy,
> And not a fieldglass sees them home,
> Or curious stop-watch prophesies:
> Only the groom, and the groom's boy,
> With bridles in the evening come.
>
> (CP, 29–30)

The horses' names are less mortal than they are, but the poet tactfully leaves implicit the expected antithesis: 'their *names* live; *they* // [die]'. The enjambement of the trailing rhyme-word 'they' into the last stanza has the effect of an anticipatory anacrusis, making us pause and take our breath – something is coming, the author is telling us. It also gives the word a dramatic, pivotal quality. At last 'they', the horses, are isolated in their own right, free to reassert their non-human identity. The unanticipated metaphorical substitution of the familiar phrase 'they have slipped their bridles' is very gratifying. But though the poem is 'opening out' emotionally at this point, the poet still keeps his distance. He can only *presume* that the horses' galloping 'must be' a sign of joy. And to guard against sentimentality, he slips in a touch of ingenious, orotund wit in the transferred epithet and mock-heroic verb of 'Or curious stop-watch prophesies', which recall the 'literary' jargon of old-fashioned racecourse-journalism.

The word 'prophesies' trails to a stop, as the reader realises that it is intransitive, and no grammatical object will follow. We are no longer curious as to *what* the stop-watch prophesied; it is of no consequence. After this eloquent pause, the voice is compelled to drop almost to a whisper for the final lines: 'Only the groom, and the groom's boy,/ With bridles in the evening come.' The elaboration of phrasing is a deliberate poeticism, lending formal elevation to the homely words – 'the groom boy', almost a title, suggesting the authentic language of the stud-farm. Also the repetition of the long vowel in 'groom' is soothing and reassuring, as is the coming of the men to the horses. The worksheets for the poem show Larkin hesitating over this rather risky effect, which like 'unmeasured meadows' could easily sound studied and oversmooth. The first rough version, 'Only the groom or the groom's boy/Bridles them home each stable night', was rewritten to avoid the crooning assonance: 'Only the groom or the stable boy/ Come down at night to call them home' (*Phoenix*, 1973/4, 100–1). In the end Larkin took the risk, and indeed compounded the 'Georgian' poeticism of the lines by inverting the word-order, placing the verb 'come' (as though some consummation were in question) at the end of the last line.

This beautiful poem is one of the most irreducible in Larkin's *œuvre*. Nevertheless it has been subjected to several more or less reductive readings. It has been mistaken for traditional pastoral, an old-fashioned, nostalgic exercise in Georgianism. A. Alvarez, for instance, patronised it as a 'genteel' work, 'elegant and unpretentious and rather beautiful in its gentle way' (26). Blake Morrison cautiously described it as in some sense 'a post-imperial poem': ' "At Grass" taps and expresses feelings of loss and regret that might, for a certain section of the British populace at least, have been unusually pronounced around 1950 (when the poem was written)' (84). Recognising that Larkin's passive, nameless horses cannot really stand as effective symbols either of imperial triumph or of imperial oppression, Morrison wisely leaves open the question of whether such post-imperial nostalgia is actually intrinsic to the poem, or merely an extrinsic element in the response of some of its readers.

More recently, however, Tom Paulin has offered an extreme version of this reading, interpreting the poem as a manifesto of literary conservatism and political prejudice. The words 'cold shade' and 'distresses', he argues, betray Larkin's affectation of 'classical' literariness; the horses are like retired generals, 'emblems of the heroic . . . observed almost by a sniper's eye'; and the line 'Only the groom, and the groom's boy' shows Larkin's reactionary devotion to the British class hierarchy (779). Deaf and heavy-footed, Paulin barges through Larkin's delicately constructed verbal devices. The sniper which he detects in the first line, for example, is the figment of simple misreading, 'pick out' becoming 'pick off' (via the military euphemism 'take out'?). Larkin's horses simply do not possess the pride and status of retired generals which Paulin's reading implies.

They are not allegorical representations of Empire, retired generals or targets for snipers. Nor do they have 'the status of superhuman ideals for restless man' (Martin, 94). They are old horses.

All these readings make the simple mistake of allegorising the horses in human terms. Alvarez, for instance, describes them as '*social* creatures of fashionable race meetings and high style' (26). But the poet is concerned precisely to deny this facile appropriation of the animals by human society. Larkin's horses feel no regret at the distance between their present anonymity and their past racetrack glories; nor does the poet feel any regret on their behalf. Certainly the long cries of 'faded, classic Junes' echo a human past whose poignant distance the poet evokes. But this sentimental, human distance only serves to point up by contrast the irreducible, mysterious, metaphysical distance between the horses' world and that of humanity, whether it be the world of the racecourse, or of the pensive onlooker trying to 'pick them out' from across the fields, or even of the groom and his boy. 'At Grass' is more a mystical poem than an ideological one.

If an ideological subtext could be detected in 'At Grass' it would not be one of imperial nostalgia, but of animal welfare, relating it to other poems in which Larkin shows an intense identification with the plight of dumb animals, such as 'Myxomatosis' and 'Take One Home for the Kiddies'. (He left a large legacy to the RSPCA in his will.) But significantly, as with his personal enthusiasm for jazz in 'Reference Back', Larkin is careful not to hang the meaning of his poem on any such narrowly personal commitment. He writes in the worksheets at one point of the 'magic of names', his interest shifting from the animals' perspective into a more general reflection on the human world. The worksheets also show him consistently refining away or rejecting his initial, very explicit moralisings over the perverse relationship between the horses and the human world: 'Their flippant names were burrs that stuck/ To gossip . . .', 'They lived in terms of men, hedged in/ By bet and bid . . .', 'But money rode them, led them in', 'Guiltlessly they galloped, yet/ Broke three people on one day' (*Phoenix*, 1973/4, 93–8). Such gauche didacticism would only have trivialised the poem's effect, and is carefully excluded from the final version in the interests of a more universal appeal.

'Wires', completed ten months later than 'At Grass', also focuses on the pathos of domestic animals in a field, but otherwise is a completely different kind of poem. It is an indication of the degree to which Larkin's creativity was driven by aesthetic and formal imperatives rather than ideological ones that these two works, with their similar central image, should be so different from each other. David Timms has made a valuable distinction between those poems by Larkin in which the central image is 'intrinsic' and those where it is not. In 'At Grass' the horses are the 'intrinsic' subject, not an allegory or metaphorical symbol. In 'Wires', as Timms says, 'The metaphor or allegory is really arbitrary' (1973/4i, 17). The cattle – conventionally less sympathetic animals than racehorses – offer merely an appropriate image of the growth from headstrong youth to boring maturity. The wit of the poem lies in the ingenious elaboration of the familiar proverbial typology: the rampant power of 'steers'; the docile passivity of 'cattle'. With this allegorical attitude towards the subject-matter goes a quite different 'freshly created universe' of verbal devices. The formal structure of 'At Grass' is progressive. The scene is set, the reflective density increases through several stanzas and then, after a pause, the poem opens out rhetorically at the end. 'Wires', in contrast, has a closed, static structure. The effect is almost comically witty, the lines being strung on that most obvious of technical devices – the rhymes:

> The widest prairies have electric fences,
> For though old cattle know they must not stray
> Young steers are always scenting purer water
> Not here but anywhere. Beyond the wires
>
> Leads them to blunder up against the wires
> Whose muscle-shredding violence gives no quarter.
> Young steers become old cattle from that day.
> Electric limits to their widest senses.

> > > > (*CP*, 48)

The rhyme-scheme is most unusual: abcd dcba, the second section being a mirror of the first. The young steers begin the poem inside the wires, but apparently unenclosed, since no rhyme is evident in the first quatrain. In their youthful masculine confidence, they are determined to 'stray' in search of the purer 'water' which they scent beyond. At the end of the first quatrain a most peculiar and ambiguous phrase embodies the naïve impracticality of their desires: 'Beyond the wires// Leads them to blunder up against the wires.' The apparently smooth enjambement into the second quatrain turns out to be brutally ironic, as the line bafflingly wrests us back to the 'wires'. At first the reader is confused, reading 'Beyond the wires' as an adverbial phrase promising a further grammatical opening out ('Beyond the wires//Lie lush green fields' perhaps). But instead of an adverbial prelude to the steers' adventures 'beyond the wires', the words turn out to be a noun phrase: a mere figment in the minds of the cattle, which leads them only to the wires. The reader is frustrated and disorientated – just as the steers are – by this puzzling conversion of adverb into noun. The ellipsis is bold, but just comprehensible, relying on a grammatical pun between the adverb 'beyond' and the noun 'beyond' (as in 'the beyond'). It could be spelled out in some such form as '[What they imagine lies] beyond the wires//Leads them to blunder up against the wires'. The closely related phrase 'the wide blue yonder' is also perhaps hinted at.

The steers have reached the wires, which – not overfancifully, perhaps – we may see as forming a two-strand fence, mimicked by the parallel lines in the middle of the poem, which rhyme uniquely on the identical word: 'wires'. The poet does not pause to contemplate the consciousnesses of the animals as he does in 'At Grass', though 'muscle-shredding' shows a wincing empathy with them. More important in this less profound poem is the rhyme scheme, which, having been activated, now briskly encloses both cattle and poem. The steers rebound from the 'wires', whose violence gives no 'quarter' (a rueful echo of the purer 'water' of line three), and 'from that day' (penultimate line) they no longer 'stray' (line two). The external 'fences' (first line) have been internalised by their electric shock into limitations on their 'senses' (last line) – which, as boring old 'cattle' rather than adventurous young 'steers', they now know better than to attempt to transcend. Though all this precise technicality of diction and rhyme is hidden beneath an apparently casual verbal surface, it does serve to make the poem into a witty equation, a *QED* of failed youthful illusions. Its neat, intellectual elegance recalls the seventeenth-century 'emblem' poem, or even those pattern poems of Herbert which make shapes to match the poem's meaning: altars or wings. Timms, writing in the early 1970s, and preferring the profounder density of such poems as 'At Grass', remarked that Larkin was writing fewer poems based on such 'extrinsic' images as 'Wires' as he matured (1973/4i,17). In fact, however, even at the height of his career Larkin still on occasion wrote such wittily closed works ('Breadfruit', 1961), and as his perspectives hardened with age he returned more frequently to such forms ('This Be The Verse', 1971; 'The View', 1972).

As Larkin's verse develops, the range of his tonal register expands. In particular, from the mid 1950s onwards, he began to elaborate a casual, demotic register, quite different from the elegiac tone adopted in different forms by most of his poems up to this time. Casual phrases and the tones of ordinary speech now frequently take the place of elegiac detachment. It is not simply a matter of the 'bad language' to which some readers occasionally take exception: 'What does it prove? Sod all', 'They fuck you up, your mum and dad.' Equally often it is simply a virtuoso casualness of manner, as polished in its effortless matching of idiom to 'the artificialities of rhyme and metre' as the most elaborate poeticism:

> At thirty-one, when some are rich
> And others dead,
> I, being neither, have a job instead . . .
> (*CP*, 69)

The successful use of such idiomatic naturalness of tone is rare in English literature. Its history is long, but discontinuous. Larkin's idioms occasionally recall the brisk vigour of the seventeenth century:

> Much wine had past with grave discourse
> Of who Fucks who and who does worse
> Such as you usually doe hear
> From those that diet at the Beare . . .
> (Rochester, 'A Ramble in Saint James's Parke', 11. 1–4)

or the offhand self-dramatisation of Byron:

> But now at thirty years my hair is gray –
> (I wonder what it will be like at forty?
> I thought of a peruk the other day –)
> My heart is not much greener; and, in short, I
> Have squander'd my whole summer while 'twas May . . .
> (*Don Juan*, Canto I. CCXIII)

No poet between Byron and Larkin achieves anything like this spontaneously personal ease of idiom, and very few poets even aim at it.

But the mature Larkin does not simply adopt different elegiac or

87

demotic registers in particular poems. He makes a point of mixing tones for original effect, or modulating from one tone to another in the course of the same poem. To use a musical/artistic analogy his work becomes more chromatic. Though some poems, 'MCMXIV' and 'This Be The Verse' for instance, stay close to a home 'key' throughout, others, such as 'Essential Beauty' and 'Vers de Société', modulate from poetic to demotic, or from comic to tragic; while a few late poems like 'Sad Steps' and 'High Windows' leap with vertiginous mannerism from one tone to another, without warning. Again, 'The View' and 'Aubade' lie at opposite poles of Larkin's emotional spectrum in the 1970s, one light and comic, the other bitterly hopeless. But in both works the poet's voice gains authority from its brief modulations away from the dominant mood. 'The View' ends with a sudden chilling anticipation of death: 'So final. And so near' (CP, 195). 'Aubade' has moments of wan humour: 'Being brave/ Lets no one off the grave' (CP, 209).

'Ambulances', a characteristic work of Larkin's high maturity, completed in 1961, displays a virtuoso ease of modulation from wit to elegiac seriousness, from colloquialism to poeticism. Though its overall tone sounds natural and unforced, analysis reveals a veritably baroque abundance of artifice. As with many of Larkin's poems, its carefully concealed formal regularity gives it an aesthetic complete-ness which is sensed rather than consciously heard. Its lines are regular iambic tetrameters and the stanzas rhyme abcbca. However, the intimate tone and the free enjambements, even between stanzas, reduce the rhymes to a quiet underlying music; while the fact that the c-rhyme in the first and last stanzas is discordantly imperfect ('absorb'/'kerb'; 'room'/'come') gives the final full rhymes in these stanzas an enhanced conclusive effect, particularly in the case of the long vowels of 'Far' and 'are' at the end. Moreover the poem broadly recreates the familiar, emotionally satisfying structure of a classical sonnet on a larger scale. The first three stanzas stand as an 'octave', describing the subject of the poem in concrete terms; the final two stanzas compose a kind of reflective 'sestet', drawing out the deeper significance of what has been described.

The diction of the poem covers a wide spectrum:

> Closed like confessionals, they thread
> Loud noons of cities, giving back
> None of the glances they absorb.

Light glossy grey, arms on a plaque,
They come to rest at any kerb:
All streets in time are visited.

Then children strewn on steps or road,
Or women coming from the shops
Past smells of different dinners, see
A wild white face that overtops
Red stretcher-blankets momently
As it is carried in and stowed . . .

(*CP*, 132)

On the one hand there is the ingenious 'poetic' circumlocution of 'thread/ Loud noons of cities', with its musical sequence of open vowels, and its transferred epithet. At the other extreme there are banal colloquial commonplaces, in virtual quotation marks ('get it whole', '*Poor soul*'), and the brutal reduction of the dying patient to a mere inanimate cargo: 'As it is carried in and stowed'. In between these extremes lies the ordinary prosaic language of 'giving back/ None of the glances' and 'women coming from the shops'.

The mixing of such widely disparate extremes of diction has a most complex and original effect. On the one hand the prosaic phrases guarantee the more elevated and 'poetic' elements, rooting them in commonplace 'reality'. But more interestingly, since the reader remains unsure as to the poem's register, many words and phrases gather added significances. 'Visited', for instance, sounds literal and inevitable. What other verb could the poet have used? But this context also activates its archaic connotations of being 'visited' by pestilence (or – in view of the religious hint in 'confessionals' – by the Inquisition?). The word 'strewn' is also ambiguous. It is still to a certain extent colloquial ('Don't leave your socks strewn about the room'), though perhaps it sounds faintly archaic or dialectal. But it is most frequent nowadays as a poeticism, and the omission of definite articles ('strewn on steps and road') points in this direction. In the context of the mixed register of the poem the reader is not forced to choose between these multiple connotations. Again 'smells' has a deliberately unpoetic effect; but the phrase 'past smells of different dinners', like 'Loud noons of cities', is poetically elaborate in structure. So 'smells' both roots the poem in commonplace reality and at the same time helps create the reflective abstraction which is essential to the elegiac effect.

As the poem progresses the prosaic expressions fall away, and the rhetoric becomes more audible. The phrase 'the solving emptiness' suggests the bleak finality of 'solving' a puzzle. It also hints at 'resolving' an issue; being 'absolved' from one's sins (by confession and repentance, or perhaps, in a secular sense, simply by death); and, of course, 'dissolving' – the physical 'dissolution' of death. There is a hint of playful wit about this effect, and the lugubriousness of the register is not without undertones. The emphatic metrical regularity of 'So permanent and blank and true', forcing the voice, as it does, to stretch out the faintly orotund 'permanent', even touches on self-conscious parody; though the wryness serves to underline the unavoidable truism of the thought rather than to mock it. A similar effect of desperately abject wit occurs three lines later in the painfully 'bad' pun: 'For *borne* away in *dead*ened air'.

The last two stanzas multiply abstract noun phrases, all stressing the growing tenuousness of the dying patient's identity. He or she (the poet is careful not to give our universal representative a gender) is no longer a person, but 'the sudden shut of loss/ Round something nearly at an end'. The grammar also ingeniously imitates the process of dissolution:

> And what cohered in it across
> The years, the unique random blend
> Of families and fashions, there
>
> At last begin to loosen.

'Begins' would be grammatically correct, but even as the poet details the blend of various elements which 'cohered' in this person, they cease to cohere and become plural. There follows one of the most hauntingly intricate constructions in Larkin's work:

> Far
> From the exchange of love to lie
> Unreachable inside a room
> The traffic parts to let go by
> Brings closer what is left to come,
> And dulls to distance all we are.
>
> (*CP*, 133)

(By the time the last line is reached 'we' have taken the place of the anonymous wild white face in the ambulance.) As with 'Beyond the wires', readers may at first be puzzled as to what exactly it is which 'Brings closer what is left to come'. What is the grammatical subject, governing the verb? It is in fact the entire infinitive noun phrase from the beginning of the sentence. It could be spelled out by disentangling the syntax: 'To lie far from the exchange of love, unreachable inside a room [which] the traffic parts to let go by, brings . . .'.

Such abstract noun phrases are one of the most intimately idiosyncratic features of Larkin's idiolect. Like any writer Larkin naturally employs his share of noun constructions. In their least complicated forms they are not grammatically unusual, though they may be very felicitous: 'Two dozen distances', 'An autumn more appropriate', 'Its bright incipience sailing above', 'the total emptiness for ever'. In these cases a noun is simply modified into a longer phrase. The characteristically 'Larkinesque' noun phrase, however, is different. It wilfully transforms a verb into a noun, sometimes by a creative use, or misuse, of grammar. 'A slight relax of air', 'the sudden shut of loss'. Larkin defines death as 'All we have done not mattering'. He tells a woman that her maiden name means 'what we feel now about you then'. Instead of 'agreeing to part' from his fiancée, he turns both verbs into nouns: 'Parting . . . was an agreement/ That I was too selfish, withdrawn,/ And easily bored to love' (*CP*, 143). Instead of acknowledging that his first encounter with a loved woman 'owed' much to previous meetings with others, he says: 'Behind . . ./ The excitement and the gratitude,/ There stood how much our meeting owed/ To other meetings, other loves' (*CP*, 205). He does not say that he feels as though he is falling as the train in which he is travelling slows down. Rather he transfers the falling into a generalised state of being: '. . . there swelled/ A sense of falling' (*CP*, 116). The traveller in 'Here' is not 'surprised' when the train 'swerves' through the unpeopled landscape into Hull. Instead the verbs are lost in noun phrases: 'Swerving east, from rich industrial shadows/ And traffic all night north; swerving through fields/ Too thin and thistled to be called meadows . . .// Gathers to the surprise of a large town' (*CP*, 136). 'Gathers' (like 'swelled' in the last example) has no active meaning on its own; it simply acts as a focus for the accumulated richness of the noun phrases which govern it and the noun phrase which it governs.

Perhaps it is impossible to argue that all these constructions perform the same function. On one level they could be seen in simple formal terms as a device of the reflective poet to fix experience in his contemplative sights. Experience is formulated in terms of states of being rather than actions. But there is more to them than this. Such noun phrases occur when Larkin's writing is at its most intensely expressive, when he seems to be searching for definitions or explanations, pondering on existence, attempting to make life stand still: to 'preserve' it. Such noun constructions are often elaborately awkward in form, and at their most intricate, as in 'Wires', 'Ambulances', and 'Here', they take the poet to the limits of grammatical tolerance. There is a sense of physical weight and tension about them. Larkin's 'fundamentally passive attitude to poetry (and life too, I suppose)' (in George Hartley, 1982, 88) finds here its most organic linguistic expression. These syntactically intricate, accumulating phrases, together with the verbs of intimate sensation which accompany them (swerve, gather, swell, loosen), seem to express a barely articulate level of consciousness where mind and physiology, consciousness and unconscious meet.

THE FIRST-PERSON POEMS

However flexible their language, the speakers in 'At Grass', 'Wires' and 'Ambulances' are, like those in 'Next, Please', 'An Arundel Tomb' and 'The Building', versions of the familiar anonymous elegist, whose long history goes back through Keats and Gray to such seventeenth-century lyricists as Herbert and Vaughan. It is, however, in the rather different poems written in the first person that Larkin's demotic register comes fully into its own. Many of Larkin's most familiar phrases include the pronouns 'I' or 'me': 'Such attics cleared of me! Such absences!', 'Hatless, I take off/ My cycle-clips in awkward reverence', 'Give me your arm, old toad', 'When I see a couple of kids/ And guess he's fucking her . . .'. The diversity of implied contexts in these poems has led some critics to interpret their speakers as dramatic personae carefully differentiated from Larkin the author. Lolette Kuby, for instance, in her early study of Larkin, shunned biographical reference as 'dangerous, since it obscures the fact that the dialogue in many of the poems is uttered by a variety of personae' (15). J. R. Watson finds in Larkin a similar self-exploration to that in Browning's dramatic monologues (348), while Simon Petch talks of the 'masks' of the *Whitsun Weddings* poems (62).

Such an approach can be useful in so far as it helps to illuminate the unique dynamic in each poem between speaker, subject and reader. But if applied too rigidly it can impose upon Larkin's most personal poems an artificial and strained irony. Petch, for instance, contrives a morally instructive reading of 'This Be The Verse' by separating the poet from his 'speaker'. According to his reading Larkin rejects the speaker's 'impoverished advice': 'Get out as early as you can,/ And don't have any kids yourself'. Petch argues that the poem uses its speaker to 'take a swipe at the very fatalism of which Larkin has been accused' (101). He goes on to offer a similar sanitised reading of 'Annus Mirabilis' as a satire on the speaker's attitude towards 'the permissive society'. There is, of course, no such didactic distance between the poet and the speaker in these works. Rather than straining to detect different personae, it is more natural to read such first-person poems as utterances of the same speaker in different, more or less ironic or self-doubting moods. When the poet was asked if 'Church Going' was a debate between poet and persona he replied: 'Well, in a way . . . I think one has to dramatize oneself a little' (in Hamilton, 74).

In only four of his mature poems does Larkin create speakers who are clearly distinguished by sex or social context from himself. In the early 'Wedding-Wind' (*CP*, 11), and the late 'Livings' (*CP*, 186), he aims at a quasi-novelistic effect, evoking the quality of the characters' lives for their own sake. The other two, 'A Study of Reading Habits' (*CP*, 131) and 'Naturally the Foundation will Bear Your Expenses' (*CP*, 134), are the only poems by Larkin which adopt the structural irony usually associated with the dramatic monologue proper. The relation between poet and speaker in each case is a tricksy and problematic one. Some critics read 'A Study of Reading Habits' as a moral attack on the false expectations and wish-fulfilment offered by pulp fiction (Petch, 64). But Larkin's evocation of the predictable sub-literature of satisfying violence and happy endings is not morally censorious in tone. Like the swaggering adventurer in 'Poetry of Departures' and the pretty girl in 'Sunny Prestatyn', the Gothic and western images in this poem ('cloak and fangs', 'the dude/ Who lets the girl down', 'the chap/ Who's yellow and keeps the store') belong to an ideal world of a kind. Only on the surface level is the poem an ironic satire on the persona who speaks its words. Larkin himself read detective stories as a boy and there is something of himself in the speaker's angry irritation that the gratifying fantasies of his early reading have failed to match adult reality. More importantly Larkin's displacement of himself into this nominally different 'character' frees him from the inhibitions of his own social and professional position. The subterfuge is quite transparent, however, and the reader savours with delight the sly transgression of a respectable librarian writing: 'Get stewed:/ Books are a load of crap'. In an interview of 1979 Larkin noted the fame of this line with a wicked satisfaction: 'If someone asked me what lines I am known for it would be the one about mum and dad or 'Books are a load of crap' – sentiments to which every bosom returns an echo, as Dr Johnson said' (*RW*, 48).

'Naturally the Foundation will Bear Your Expenses' offers a more complex problem, and has been widely misread. Larkin complained: 'I've never written a poem that has been less understood' (in Hamilton, 76). First-time readers still find its mixed satirical and euphoric tone difficult to interpret, confused by the poet's ambiguous attitude to his speaker. On the one hand the poem is a satire on the cynical, name-dropping academic, revelling in his ability to 'outsoar' the rest of us on his academic 'freebie'. On the other hand, like 'Poetry of Departures' and 'Toads' it fantasises one of those exhilarating but insubstantial escapes from responsibility which abound in Larkin's work. Discussion has been complicated by Larkin's apparent endorsement in an early interview of a reductive ideological version of the poem. Finding to his embarrassment that early readers were taking the poem to be simple left-wing satire ('rather hard on the Queen'), or condemning it as unsuccessful light verse (in Hamilton, 76), Larkin gratefully approved John Wain's reading of the work as a 'serious' topical satire.

Wain had written: 'What comes through is a deep antipathy to the *New Statesman* intellectual with his automatic contempt for the slow, devious logic of the English popular mind, his opportunism which proceeds by "contacts", and his glossy internationalism, which makes him feel that his fate is not really bound up with England's' (172). Leaving aside the difficulty of locating 'the slow, devious logic of the English popular mind' anywhere in Larkin's poem, the major problem with this reading is that the poem's tone fails to convey the kind of moral severity which Wain discovers in it. Moreover, the explanation with which Larkin follows his praise of Wain seems to hint at a milder reading: 'Certainly it was a dig at the middleman who gives a lot of talks to America and then brushes them up and does them on the Third and then brushes them up again and puts them out as a book with Chatto' (in Hamilton, 76). There is a concessiveness in that 'Certainly . . .', as though Larkin did not wish to follow Wain all the way.

It is clear enough, however, that on one level at least the poem is a 'dig' at an academic careerist, though the severity of its satire may be doubted. But is it also politically motivated, as Wain implies? The argument centres on the reference to the Armistice Day ceremony:

> Crowds, colourless and careworn,
>   Had made my taxi late,
> Yet not till I was airborne
>   Did I recall the date –
> That day when Queen and Minister
>   And Band of Guards and all
> Still act their solemn-sinister
>   Wreath-rubbish in Whitehall.
>
> It used to make me throw up,
>   These mawkish nursery games:
> O when will England grow up?
>   (*CP*, 134)

The speaker's anger at the ceremonial is awkwardly expressed, suggesting real emotion. If Larkin intended to satirise the speaker's attitude one might have expected glib heartlessness, rather than this defensive, embarrassed bluster. John Wain, J. R. Watson, Simon Petch and Terry Whalen all assert that Larkin respects the Armistice Day ceremony and wishes his readers to take the side of the crowds against the speaker. The single phrase 'colourless and careworn' is made on this reading to bear an implausibly heavy burden of implied 'compassion' (Whalen, 80) for the Armistice Day crowds. Petch feels that the speaker's 'lack of essential seriousness' leads the reader to 'assume the value the poet places on the service' (62–3). The other critics import their own pieties into the poem in order to supply Larkin's omission. Wain rhapsodises that Larkin 'identifies with the puzzled, mournful crowds . . . trying in an inarticulate fashion to show that, while they cannot comprehend the nature of the earthquake that was the First World War, they still wish to show some feeling about the men who died in it' (172). Watson waxes indignant: 'the thought of Larkin himself actually regarding a Remembrance Day service as "solemn-sinister/ Wreath-rubbish" is so wrong as to be offensive, and the suggestion tells us more about the minds of the critics than anything else' (349).

These commentators confuse genuine feeling for the war-dead with reverence for the public rituals in which royalty and politicians, in the name of 'the Nation', commemorate them. This is not a mistake which Wilfred Owen or Siegfried Sassoon would have made. Nor does Larkin. Immediately after praising Wain's interpretation he goes on plaintively to defend the speaker's attitude in the poem: 'Why he should be blamed for not sympathising with the crowds on Armistice Day, I don't quite know' (in Hamilton, 76). Elsewhere Larkin expresses loathing for full dress occasions and ceremonial claptrap (his reference to Churchill and the King 'blathering out of turn' on VE-Day for instance). It may be questioned, then, whether Larkin's speaker is, after all, the creation of coherent ideological satire. Does Larkin's 'dig' at his academic careerism develop into a serious satire on his treasonable left-wing contempt for his country's 'noble dead'? The reference to Forster, the liberal homosexual who, in conservative demonology, 'corrupted' the Cambridge traitors, might just possibly point to such an interpretation (Wain and Petch see Forster as a symbol of true human feeling in the poem). It seems more likely however that in describing the Armistice Day ceremonial Larkin's own edgy iconoclasm has taken over, and at this point the speaker slips uneasily from satirised character to poet's mouthpiece.

His outburst over, the speaker relaxes again into the shallow exuberance with which the poem began. It is as easy to find his flippancy refreshing as repellent, and it is not surprising that so many readers fail to take the poem's satire seriously. Irresponsible rhymes like 'Minister/ sinister', 'throw up/ grow up', 'Auster/ Forster', 'Lal/ pal', function not as destructive cuts of the satirist's knife; they give imaginative life to the poem. And the poet's supposed moral disgust is quite lost in the engaging euphoria of the final line ('My contact and my pal'), with its simple celebration of the superficalities of expense-account jaunting. Larkin's creative imagination has transcended his mildly satirical intention, and the exhilaration of his persona has hijacked the poem. Or, in Freudian terms, a slippery imaginative irony has cheated the poet's repressive superego (a responsible Tory librarian), and allowed the voice of his id (an anarchic free spirit) to be heard through the superego's show of moral satire. Larkin could be said to be writing not like Browning, in the voice of an ironic persona, but like Yeats, in the voice of his 'mask' or opposite. He is not as ironically distanced from his character as he seems. This speaker is only a slightly more fictionally fantasised version of the 'I' of his other poems.

The dynamic of Larkin's first-person works derives, not from any satire against others, but from the poet's quarrel with himself. Satire, in the usual sense, inhabits only the most superficial levels of his imagination. His self-satire is however profound. The most characteristic form of Larkin's first-person poems is an argument over his role in life. Alternative options are reviewed, often in vivid stereotypical form, and the poet defends his position with bitter passion or comic equanimity, or a mixture of both. 'Reasons for Attendance' and 'Poetry of Departures', completed within a month of each other at the end of 1953 and the beginning of 1954, show Larkin adjusting the dramatic context and register of his speaking voice to generate quite different self-dramatisations. In 'Reasons for Attendance', the speaker's defence of his lonely vocation to 'attend' to the 'rough-tongued bell' of art, rather than join in the dance of the couples, is embarrassed and insecure. His sense of his own role is not as certain as he claims, and his casual, insouciant tone is unconvincing:

> Why be out here?
> But then, why be in there? Sex, yes, but what
> Is sex? Surely, to think the lion's share
> Of happiness is found by couples – sheer
>
> Inaccuracy, as far as I'm concerned.
> What calls me is that lifted, rough-tongued bell
> (Art, if you like) whose individual sound
> Insists I too am individual.
> It speaks; I hear; others may hear as well . . .
>
> (*CP*, 80)

When he refers to his artistic vocation the sulky argumentativeness gives way to a more confident tone. But the speaker remains uneasy, attempting to disarm the anticipated ridicule of his audience with parentheses and qualifications – '(Art, if you like)'. The poem ends on an ironic 'take it or leave it' note:

97

> Therefore I stay outside,
> Believing this; and they maul to and fro,
> Believing that; and both are satisfied,
> If no one has misjudged himself. Or lied.

'Poetry of Departures' shows a witty inversion of the emotional pattern of 'Reasons for Attendance'. In the earlier poem, the speaker feels impelled to reject the normal dance of courtship and marriage ('The wonderful feel of girls') and to obey the lonely call of 'Art'. The speaker of 'Poetry of Departures', in contrast, rejects the call of popular romance, to relapse into the contemptible domestic security of his humdrum and 'Reprehensibly perfect' life. The recasting of the art versus life theme in these comic terms makes this a lighter, more public poem. Here the conflicting registers are no longer tangled together as in the earlier work, but neatly separated off by the use of italics. The dominant voice is the detached commentary of the speaker, into which is inserted a series of colloquial quotations summarising the fantasy of casual glamour which he could – he would like to believe – turn into reality at any time if the mood took him:

> *He walked out on the whole crowd*
> Leaves me flushed and stirred,
> Like *Then she undid her dress*
> Or *Take that you bastard*;
> Surely I can, if he did?
>
> (*CP*, 85)

The italicised phrases have something of the vivid force of cultural icons, like the isolated frames of comic strips in the pop-art paintings of Roy Lichtenstein. Out of their sub-literary context they take on a new comic-pathetic resonance. But the poet does not simply isolate these clichés; he creatively transforms them. The language in which the swashbuckling pirate is described is strangely original:

> But I'd go today,
>
> Yes, swagger the nut-strewn roads,
> Crouch in the fo'c'sle
> Stubbly with goodness . . .
>
> (*CP*, 85)

Though the phrases here *sound* vaguely familiar ('the nut-strewn roads', 'Stubbly with goodness'), and immediately perform their function in conjuring up some Technicolor Gregory Peck or Tony Curtis, they are in fact not familiar verbal clichés. Rather they are a poetic apotheosis of the cliché. 'Stubbly with goodness' has no possible meaning outside the context of this poem. It possesses a similarly memorable uniqueness to 'All but the unmolesting meadows' in 'At Grass'. It sticks in the mind, almost like a freshly minted proverb.

Larkin's most engaging comic poems are meditations on familiar role-models of this kind. The speaker presents himself characteristically as disgruntled, rather than anguished, and the humour is lightly self-mocking. In his recorded reading of 'Toads' (also completed in 1954), Larkin's voice begins in an ineffectual whine, then modulates to mock-heroic lugubriousness, as he wickedly clashes colloquial 'bad language' against one of the most classically beautiful lines in Shakespeare's *The Tempest*:

> Ah, were I courageous enough
> To shout *Stuff your pension*!
> But I know, all too well, that's the stuff
> That dreams are made on . . .
>
> (*CP*, 89)

The comic effect of this casually mixed register is even more polished and assured in 'Toads Revisited', completed more than eight years later in 1962 (*CP*, 147–8). The very title is a self-mocking literary joke. The poet, deeming 'Toads' to have become a 'classic' in the years since its publication, now produces a sequel such as followed other great classics of the past: 'Yarrow Revisited' (Wordsworth), or 'Locksley Hall Sixty Years After' (Tennyson). The resulting collocation – 'Toads Revisited' – is bewitchingly surreal – another one of those phrases which remain unforgettable because of their unique oddity. The initial image of work as a toad squatting on our lives is perhaps the least remarkable element in these whimsical, comic-serious meditations. An interviewer once asked Larkin the mind-boggling question: 'How did you arrive upon the image of a toad for work or labour?' He replied with the same self-referential ebullience as that in the poems: 'Sheer genius' (*RW*, 74).

The ripest (even overripe) tones of this argumentative, self-satiric voice, in Larkin's work, are heard in 'The Life with a Hole in it', completed in 1974 on the day before his fifty-second birthday. This is Larkin's self-dramatisation at a mannerist extreme, the kind of near self-parody that has been called 'a fine performance on the Larkin' in contrast with the richer, more organic earlier poems (Bayley, 158). Again the title itself sums up the poem's mood: in this case a pungent mixture of bad temper and despair, with its bitter offhand reference to the advertisement for Polo mints: 'The mint with the hole'. The unusually elaborate, interwoven rhyme-scheme (abcbaddc) is wantonly abused. It could easily have been the vehicle for complex music, but this is spoiled by the shortness of the rough trimeter lines, by the casual half-rhymes, and most of all by the metre which is a free mix of iambs and anapaests, frequently breaking into a jogging rant:

> When I throw back my head and howl
> People (women mostly) say
> *But you've always done what you want,*
> *You always get your own way*
> – A perfectly vile and foul
> Inversion of all that's been.
> What the old ratbags mean
> Is I've never done what I don't.
>
> (*CP*, 202)

The threefold alliteration on the aspirated 'h' in line 1 ('When', 'head', 'howl') is crude and melodramatic, and the first two feet are anapaests (analogous to triplets in music) tumbling out with vehemence and then opening out into the final iamb:

$$\overset{x\ x\ /}{\text{When I throw}} \mid \overset{x\ x\ /}{\text{back my head}} \mid \overset{x\ /}{\text{and howl}} \dots$$

It is an exaggerated effect like the physical gesture it describes. The next line strikes a note of sudden prickly briskness by reining in the metre to clipped regular trochees, in an abrupt shift from a rising to a falling metre. The aside – '(women mostly)' – demands to be read with a contemptuous dip in the voice, the placing of the women in parentheses being a deliberate tetchy snub. The quoted words of the women are to be read in a sarcastic mimicking whine, and their second line repeats the pattern of the first to imply a nagging repetitiveness. Each line has a concluding anapaest and repeats the see-saw pattern 'you've always . . . you . . ./ You always . . . your', the heaviest stress falling insistently on the first syllable of 'always' in both cases.

In the next stanza the speaker's focus shifts and it begins to emerge that what is really putting him so out of temper is not the whining 'old ratbags', but the fact that he feels he has missed out on something. As they say, he *ought* to be satisfied, but he isn't, and really has no ready answer to their complaint – hence the frustrated bluster. With crude vehemence he places himself between two familiar Larkinesque images of male destiny: the wealthy novelist-playboy of his fantasy, and the dutiful downtrodden husband of his fears. But the sense of imaginative pleasure Larkin once felt in fantasising the former destiny is now as dead as his sense of blessed release in having avoided the latter. Both stereotypes demonstrate their own threadbare crudity in their thumping anapaestic sequences and utterly ghastly alliterations and rhymes ('words/ birds', 'sod/ pod'; 'the shit in the shuttered château', 'Between bathing and booze and birds', 'that spectacled schoolteaching sod'). This is brilliantly effective 'bad' writing. The poet presents himself as flailing about, unhappily aware that his exasperation is out of proportion to its apparent occasion.

The third stanza attempts to philosophise the poem's lesson and finally seems to approach the real source of the poet's anger. Life is an irresolvable struggle between one's id ('Your wants'), one's superego ('the world's for you') and 'The unbeatable slow machine/ That brings what you'll get'. But it is ultimately not the 'hollow stasis' around which these forces strain which really worries the speaker. It is simply the passing of time: 'Days sift down it constantly. Years.' Even at its most excessive and histrionic Larkin's angry, bad-mannered demotic register is ready at a touch to modulate into the sombre dignity of elegy. Here in this virtuoso late work the transition is left until the very last line. Indeed the full poignancy of its effect is not accomplished until the very end of the poem, with the sudden quiet pensiveness of that last, effortlessly elliptical single-word sentence: 'Years'.

4

'A real girl in a real place'

SEX AND LOVE

S E X

Among the poems which Larkin wrote during his first burst of mature poetic creativity are the companion pieces 'Two Portraits of Sex', both completed in March 1950 when he was 27 years old. Their subtitles, 'Oils' and 'Etching', relating them to techniques in pictorial art, suggest a deliberate experiment in antithetical styles: on the one hand the colour and texture of oil-paint, and on the other the black-and-white austerity of an etching. There were lessons to be learnt from the relative success of the two resulting poems. 'Oils', with its mythic evocation of life-juices, aims at the full-blooded grandeur of an ambitious oil-painting, beginning in the garden of Eden and developing a series of elaborate meta-phorical variations. It shows Larkin straining to 'jack [him]self up to a concept of poetry that lay outside [his] own life' (*RW*, 175). Its tone is religious and declamatory, strangely echoing George Herbert's sonnet 'Prayer':

> Sun. Tree. Beginning. God in a thicket. Crown.
> Never-abdicated constellation. Blood.
> Barn-clutch of life. Trigger of the future.
> Magic weed the doctor shakes in the dance.

Many rains and many rivers, making one river.
Password. Installation. Root of tongues.

(*CP*, 36)

The theme, sex as the source of all life, is a simpler version of that of Yeats's 'Leda and the Swan', while the poem's explicit symbolic vocabulary, its bold elliptical style, and its awed reverence of tone, recall at times both Hopkins and Dylan Thomas. But the literary influences are not fused together successfully, and the poem's prophetic manner lacks assurance:

Working-place to which the small seed is guided,
Inlet unvisited by marine biologist,
Entire alternative in man and woman
Opening at a touch like a water-flower,
New voice saying new words at a new speed
From which the future erupts like struck oil . . .

(*CP*, 36)

The kinetic slowing up of the penultimate line here with its emphatic repetitive phrases –

/ \ / x / \ x x / \
New voice saying new words at a new speed

– is bold and strange. But the translation of sexual intercourse into 'archetypal' imagery – seeds, inlets, opening flowers, erupting oil – is embarrassingly fervent in tone. The reader may even suspect that the poet has dropped in the grotesquely incongruous 'marine biologist' as a sly joke, mocking his own pretentiousness. It is only at the end of the poem, when the rhetorical inflation falters, that an authentic note is struck. Sacramental religiosity subsides, to be replaced by a grim Larkinesque bitterness at the tyranny of sexual desire, expressed with monosyllabic finality: 'No one can tear your thread out of himself./ No one can tie you down or set you free.'

Not surprisingly this grammatically extreme, and in some details obscure, exercise in experimental 'modernism' was not included in *The Less Deceived*. Larkin did however consider its companion piece worthy to appear in his first mature collection, though with the coarse sexual pun of its title (Etching/ itching) replaced by a more teasingly elusive word-play. The new title, 'Dry-Point', is the technical term for a kind of engraving, but it also suggests the sterile aridity (dry point) of post-orgasmic depression. A hint of vulgar raucousness lurks below the beautiful surface in the sly equation of engraving tool with penis (compare the public house toast: 'here's lead in your pencil'):

> Endlessly, time-honoured irritant,
> A bubble is restively forming at your tip.
> Burst it as fast as we can –
> It will grow again, until we begin dying.
> Silently it inflates, till we're enclosed
> And forced to start the struggle to get out:
> Bestial, intent, real.
> The wet spark comes, the bright blown walls collapse. . . .
>
> (*CP*, 36–7)

The subject of the poem is the same as that of 'Oils': sex as an inescapable biological force whose imperious demands are coterminous with life itself. But in this case uneasy echoes of earlier poets are absent, and the tone is entirely Larkin's own: exquisitely modulated, secular, without illusions. This is by no means verse for 'the common man', however; and not merely because of its intimate sexual subject matter. Stylistically it remains as thoroughly 'symbolist' a poem as its original companion piece. The graphic physical description of tumescence which is constantly implied never becomes crudely explicit, and works in its own right as an evocation of less simply physical emotions. (Indeed some early critics completely missed the physical reference of the poem: see George Hartley 1973/4, 105–9). The evocation of orgasm in the last line, for instance, is delicate and original in comparison with the ecstatic Hopkinsesque eruption of 'struck oil' in 'Oils'. The contrived oxymoron ('wet spark'), and the psychologically accurate vagueness of the imagery ('the bright blown walls collapse') create the kind of exact objective correlative of emotion sought by the poets of the Symbolist and Imagist movements, while not sounding at all derivative in tone or manner.

Few poets write so intimately about sexual activity as a biological affair between themselves and their own bodies. If we are to seek the tradition to which the poem belongs, or at least 'intertextual' parallels to it, they are perhaps to be found in Shakespeare's Sonnet 129, on lust, 'Th'expense of spirit in a waste of shame', and the latter part of Rochester's famous poem on premature ejaculation, 'The Imperfect Enjoyment'. All three poets evoke the demanding, biological nature of male sexual desire. They all address their own flesh in 'irritation', criticising it for its disappointments, evoking in particular the spent hopelessness which follows orgasm. For Shakespeare 'lust' is 'A bliss in proof, and prov'd, a very woe'. Rochester, having failed his mistress by his premature ejaculation, berates his unreliable penis with comic dismay, 'Shrunk up, and Sapless, like a wither'd *Flow'r*' (1.45). For Larkin the bursting of the bubble is also the occasion for mock-heroic despair, but now expressed in extravagant, surrealist visions of post-orgasmic *tristesse*:

> But what sad scapes we cannot turn from then:
> What ashen hills! what salted, shrunken lakes!
> How leaden the ring looks,
> Birmingham magic all discredited . . .
>
> (*CP*, 37)

Until Larkin's generation 'Brummagem-ware' was still a byword for cheap and showy goods, particularly jewellery, and this free-floating image of a wedding-ring hints at the larger social disappointments of marriage and domesticity which lie behind the merely physical disappointment of orgasm.

The endings of the three poems are similarly bleak, though Larkin develops an original and characteristic variation. Shakespeare, with Elizabethan moral sententiousness, ruefully admits: 'yet none knows well/ To shun the heaven that leads men to this hell.' Rochester ends with the shocking wish that his penis be punished for its indiscipline by the 'rav'nous chancres' (ulcers) of syphilis. Larkin's ending in contrast shifts abruptly to an aesthete's yearning for escape. The disappointment of sex serves only to intensify his vision of detached, sexless, aesthetic stasis, which – illogically, yet with perfect psychological plausibility – the failure of the flesh seems to validate and to intensify:

> And how remote that bare and sunscrubbed room,
> Intensely far, that padlocked cube of light
> We neither define nor prove,

Where you, we dream, obtain no right of entry.

(*CP*, 37)

'Dry-Point' offers Larkin's most extreme formulation of the familiar antithesis of 'flesh' versus 'spirit', though in Larkin's version there is no escape from the physical world. The final image of transcendence, far from asserting some 'spiritual' alternative to the world of the flesh, declares itself to be merely the product of a hopeless yearning to escape from inescapable reality.

Larkin's poem is extreme, in comparison with Shakespeare's and Rochester's, in its virtual exclusion (apart from the sour allusion to the wedding-ring) of women. Larkin was unillusioned, even at an early age, about the nature of his sexuality, and his relationships with women are not marked by any of the customary blends of desire with social romance or spiritual idealism. In a letter written in 1946 the 23-year-old Larkin comments on a recent visit to Oxford:

> Everybody there seemed to be having a better time than I am. —— in particular is busily shagging a girl – a new girl – at every opportunity, which makes me envious: never think I dispute the desirability of women. My quarrel is that their ['its' deleted] attainment is only possibly [*sic*] on such unwelcome terms. (18.vi.46)

It was more than a careless slip which caused the poet to write 'its' in the last sentence here, and then correct it to 'their'. Sex and women are separate categories in his mind, and it is the unfortunate interdependence of 'it' and 'them' which is the cause of his unhappy situation. He expressed the distinction with comic brutality in a letter to Amis in which he begrudged the waste of money involved in taking girls out: 'I don't – I *don't* – want to . . . spend circa £5 when I can toss off in five minutes, free, and have the rest of the evening to myself' (1991, 61). Larkin's view of sexuality is very different in this respect from that of his great twentieth-century predecessors, Yeats and Eliot.

SEXUAL POLITICS

Larkin's characteristic view of sex as first and foremost a solipsistic problem of his own body has the paradoxical effect of freeing his

attitudes towards women from the cruder kinds of sexual politics. In
'Lines on a Young Lady's Photograph Album' Larkin strikes a tone
quite inconceivable in a poem by Yeats or Eliot, in his address to the
'Faithful and disappointing' art of photography:

> what grace
> Your candour thus confers upon her face!
> How overwhelmingly persuades
> That this is a real girl in a real place,
>
> In every sense empirically true!
>
> (*CP*, 71-2)

The maximum memorable emphasis is given to the crucial phrase,
by freely distorting the metre and playing on the virtual disyllabic
pronunciation of 'real':

> x /(x) / x x /(x) /
> a real girl in a real place. . .

The poet celebrates the girl's independent, irreducible reality; the
epiphany which she offers is secular, 'empirically true!'. Though the
women in Larkin's poems arouse his sexual desires and anxieties, as
the girl does here, they never become mere embodiments of his
subjective emotions. They remain empirically 'real'. In contrast,
both Yeats and Eliot generate archetypes of femaleness. Yeats
creates a Romantic fusion of flesh and spirit in the form of the
mythified Maud Gonne, the object of his physical desire and at the
same time the embodiment of aesthetic Beauty and spiritual
transcendence. T. S. Eliot reflects a more ancient pre-Romantic
pattern, separating the flesh and the spirit into opposing female
symbols. He juxtaposes Whores: the promiscuous typist, Cleopatra
and the Thames Maidens of *The Waste Land*; and Virgins: Mary,
and the spiritual and sexless medieval 'Lady' of *Ash Wednesday*.
Behind Yeats's Helen of Troy, and behind Eliot's hyacinth girl and
'Lady of silences', stand metaphysical or religious systems with
which Larkin will have no truck.

A large proportion of Larkin's poems concerned with relations
between the sexes could be characterised as satires or elegies on the
gulf between the mythic ideals of our sexual dreams and the
empirical reality out of which they are constructed. The gender roles

which Larkin projects usually reflect untransformed social specifics, rather than being taken from what he irreverently called the 'common myth-kitty' (*RW*, 79). Instead of creating archetypes, Larkin dramatises and ironises upon stereotypes. His images of women tend to be the products not of poetic myth, but of novelistic realism or popular folklore. In his work the sexual caricatures of the public house and the tennis club, the 'bosomy English rose', and the 'friend in specs' (*CP*, 143), replace Helen of Troy and Dante's Beatrice. It could be argued that such stereotypes, like the dowdy and prudish Margaret and the sexually promising Christine of *Lucky Jim*, merely offer a different, equally pernicious sexist mythography. But this would be to ignore the complexity of Larkin's use of these types. He does not trust them. They are a means of approaching reality, not the reality itself. His poems dramatise rather than embody them. We are presented not simply with the titillating transvestism of the girl 'in a trilby hat', but also with the poet's 'swivel eye' leering at her 'Faintly disturbing' image in her photograph album (*CP*, 71). Larkin's images of women possess neither the rhetorical solemnity which Yeats and Eliot give to theirs, nor the enthusiastic imaginative commitment which Amis gives to his. Instead he shows something of the insistent self-parody of a James Joyce. Like Joyce he has no belief in ideological systems, either social or sexual. The truth of his poems is a matter of the conflicting play of subjectivities.

This play of subjectivities is at its most strenuous in the intensely personal works written in the early 1950s in the wake of his failed engagement. In these poems the crudest stereotypes of pusillanimous female timidity and questing male aggression are pitted against each other in a bitter war of the sexes. The most extreme poem in this group is 'The Less Deceived' (later retitled 'Deceptions' when its original title was transferred to the 1955 volume), written in February 1950. Unusually for Larkin, this poem takes its characters of Victorian rapist and victim ready-made from an earlier book, Henry Mayhew's *London Labour and the London Poor*, Volume IV (1862), and this specific reliance on a classic sociological text seems part of a strategic attempt by the poet to displace or sublimate his painful personal emotion. The stark, low-life brutality of Mayhew's story serves as an imaginative vehicle for Larkin's contradictory feelings of resentment, anger and self-contempt. The pattern of violation seen at the end of *A Girl in Winter* is repeated in a more extreme form, as the poet seeks to expiate his sense of guilt through an expression of sympathy with the victim in Mayhew's text.

A summary of Mayhew's account helps to show why it caught Larkin's imagination, and how the original moral and sexual categories of the Victorian context are transformed in the poem, and given new meanings. Mayhew's approach is rigorously objective and sociological. The woman is offered as a typical case-history, a representative of that 'lowest class of women, who prostitute themselves for a shilling or less . . . a woman over forty, shabbily dressed, and with a disreputable, unprepossessing appearance'. The Victorian sociologist informs us quaintly that she volunteered her statement 'for a consideration of a spirituous nature'. His sympathy for her is lost in his sexist double standard: 'This woman's tale is a condensation of the philosophy of sinning' (241). She was, as she told Mayhew, the daughter of a tenant-farmer in Dorset, who had come to London to visit an aunt 'when I was quite a gal, not above sixteen, I dessay'. Shortly after her arrival, and still totally innocent, she was lured by a plausible man into a brothel, where she was drugged and raped. It is important to the understanding of Larkin's poem to note that the man is not a low-life pimp engaged in his trade, but a middle-class voluptuary in search of new experience:

> When I became quiet I received a visit from my seducer, in whom I had placed so much silly confidence. He talked very kindly to me, but I would not listen to him for some time. He came several times to see me, and at last said he would take me away if I liked, and give me a house of my own. Finally, finding how hopeless all was I agreed to his proposal and he allowed me four pounds a week. This went on for some months, till he was tired of me, when he threw me over for some one else. There is always as good fish in the sea as ever came out of it, and this I soon discovered.
> Then for some years – ten years, till I was six-and-twenty – I went through all the changes of a gay lady's life . . . .
> (Mayhew, 240)

In Larkin's poem the woman regains her dignity and of course loses her Victorian moral context. Moreover the poet annihilates the longer perspective by which the prostitute softens her pain and reduces her violation to the commonplace. Instead he focuses with vivid emotional intensity on the moment of greatest stress in Mayhew's text, when the girl first realises her situation:

> 'Of course I was drugged, and so heavily
> I did not regain my consciousness till the
> next morning. I was horrified to discover
> that I had been ruined, and for some days
> I was inconsolable, and cried like a child
> to be killed or sent back to my aunt.'
> Mayhew, *London Labour and the London
> Poor*

> Even so distant, I can taste the grief,
> Bitter and sharp with stalks, he made you gulp.
> The sun's occasional print, the brisk brief
> Worry of wheels along the street outside
> Where bridal London bows the other way . . .
>
> (*CP*, 32)

The poet's intimate address to the girl, dramatically placed at the point immediately following her 'ruin', also has the effect of giving an intensely personal tone to his relationship with her, distant though she is. The 'I' in the first line is insistent, almost as though he fears that his sympathy might be doubted. But the most telling modification of Mayhew's perspective comes at the end of Larkin's poem, which suddenly shifts in point of view from the girl to the rapist. Mayhew occupied himself entirely with the victim. The rapist remained a conventional villain, a mere cypher. Larkin in contrast, intrudes, in the first person, upon the woman's grief, in order to offer a gauche apology on her rapist's behalf:

> Slums, years, have buried you. I would not dare
> Console you if I could. What can be said,
> Except that suffering is exact, but where
> Desire takes charge, readings will grow erratic?
> For you would hardly care
> That you were less deceived, out on that bed,
> Than he was, stumbling up the breathless stair
> To burst into fulfilment's desolate attic.
>
> (*CP*, 32)

The poet, it seems, detects in this man's refusal to submit to the conventions of 'bridal London' an idealism as vulnerable as the girl's conventional honour, and ultimately doomed to even greater and more tragic disappointment. Indeed, she is 'less deceived' by the rape inflicted upon her than her 'deceiver' is by his own quest for the ultimate illusory sexual 'fulfilment'. The rapist, reinterpreted by the poet as an eternally disappointed idealist, vies for the reader's sympathy with the girl, drugged, raped and betrayed into prostitution by the man she trusted.

Such defensive concern for the rapist's self-deception may seem as shocking a complicity with his crime as was Mayhew's lack of moral interest in him. The poem can be accused of offering 'a masculine view of rape', and the poet's statement that 'where/ Desire takes charge, readings will grow erratic', can be condemned as attempting 'to shift the responsibility for this fundamental masculine crime onto some abstract power beyond actual men and women' (Holderness 1989ii, 127). It is easy to share Janice Rossen's dissatisfaction with the willingness of many critics to be persuaded by Larkin's apparent 'argument':

> A question such as 'Is it really worse for the rapist because he is less undeceived than the girl is?' seems academic and cruel on the critic's part, if this is indeed what the poet is proposing. (Rossen, 89)

She concludes that the poem's 'callousness . . . ought at the least to be seen as problematic – and as a limitation in Larkin's art' (89–90). Such criticisms seem to carry conviction. However Rossen's qualifying phrase ('if this is indeed what the poet is proposing') points to a saving element: namely the poet's manifest embarrassment and distress. Even as he hesitantly articulates his brutally masculine argument, he admits the emotional falseness of his position: 'I would not dare/ Console you if I could . . ./ For you would hardly care . . .'. There is a grim moral honesty in the poet's acknowledgement that he himself 'feels, most strongly, not the suffering, but the disgusting violence of male desire and he is therefore only capable of a complete identification with the blind frustrated man' (Goode, 134). Nevertheless there is a desperation in the poet's insistence that beyond the immediate sexual politics of rape, the man also is a victim. The tone is helpless and humble, suggesting perhaps that this is a more personal poem than it at first seems.

111

The root of the problem is the poem's strange mixture of detached distance and vivid immediacy. The uncharacteristically displaced central image, borrowed from a very different text, seems to show a concern on the poet's part to push the act of masculine violence safely into the distance ('Slums, years, have buried you'). Yet paradoxically this distance seems to make his own feelings of guilt over this violence even more anxious and urgent ('Even so distant, I can taste . . .'). His insistent apologies to this long-dead Victorian woman seem artificial, almost in bad faith. One may suspect that the image of rape is an extreme metaphor for his immediate personal feelings concerning his engagement, hence the histrionic tortuousness of his tone. Viewed in this light the poem's unhappy apology for the rapist may appear less simply sexist than it seems at first sight. Moreover the poem's original, riddling title, 'The Less Deceived', suggests an even more devious personal subtext, and an even more remote literary displacement of the poet's emotion. Its allusion, as Larkin revealed, is to Shakespeare's *Hamlet*. The Prince declares 'I loved you not', and Ophelia replies 'I was the more deceived' (Jean Hartley, 74). This echo, which would not have been detectable without the poet's help, perhaps indicates a private Freudian joke on his part, even a wry cynicism about his own self-dramatising contortions in the poem. The poet is perhaps here acknowledging to himself that, like some mock-heroic Prince of Denmark, he was also at this time driving his beloved to distraction by his moody antics following the death of his father.

'If, My Darling', completed three months after 'The Less Deceived', again pits troubling female innocence against interesting male depravity. Here however the antithesis is expressed not in terms of Victorian deceiver and victim, but of the stereotypes of post-war sexual folklore. The poem reads rather like the resentful sexual politicking of a poetic Jim Dixon, fending off a Margaret who is determined to get him to marry and 'settle down'. Her bourgeois myth of paradise is encapsulated in wickedly telling details: mahogany sideboards, the lockable decanter ('tantalus'), a cosy fender-seat and the books reserved for Sunday:

> If my darling were once to decide
> Not to stop at my eyes,
> But to jump, like Alice, with floating skirt into my head,
>
> She would find no tables and chairs,

No mahogany claw-footed sideboards,
No undisturbed embers;

The tantalus would not be filled, nor the fender-seat cosy,
Nor the shelves stuffed with small-printed books for the
Sabbath . . .
(*CP*, 41)

This pathetic feminine vision of security is brutally contradicted by
an assertion of male restlessness and intellectual scepticism. Her
substantial and coherent illusion is corrected by his incoherent and
dissatisfying reality. There is a savage relish about the attack on his
darling's expectations in the second part, and the poet's own version
of the inside of his head seems designed as much to offend her as to
refute her banal expectations:

She would also remark
The unwholesome floor, as it might be the skin of a grave,

From which ascends an adhesive sense of betrayal,
A Grecian statue kicked in the privates, money,
A swill-tub of finer feelings. But most of all

She'd be stopping her ears against the incessant recital
Intoned by reality, larded with technical terms,
Each one double-yolked with meaning and meaning's
rebuttal:

For the skirl of that bulletin unpicks the world like a knot,
And to hear how the past is past and the future neuter
Might knock my darling off her unpriceable pivot.
(*CP*, 41)

But though the poet may be less deceived than his darling, the
relation between them is still essentially that of a grammatical
comparative. He has no liberating 'truth' with which to refute her
illusion, and this gives his attempt to undeceive her something of a
bad conscience. The gothic unwholesomeness which he attributes to
himself is overpitched. At times he seems almost to be losing control
of his medium. There is sulky petulance in his placing of his 'finer
feelings' in a 'swill-tub'. With a sense of miserable exasperation the

images collapse into desultory truculence and mixed metaphor. Double-yolked technical terms sound far-fetched rather than sinister. Readers may rack their brains as to how on earth a 'bulletin' can 'skirl', and how this skirling can 'unpick' a 'knot'. The word-play in 'future neuter' is wanly witty, but in a contrived way, while the phrase 'unpriceable pivot' (why 'pivot'?) awkwardly betrays itself as a forced variation on some more idiomatic phrase (such as 'precious pedestal'). Nevertheless the very rhetorical insecurity of the poem is emotionally effective in a way it would not have been had its basic male-triumphalist intention been followed through with more assurance. Self-criticism vies with self-exoneration. The poet has set out to launch a simple misogynistic attack on his darling's delusions; instead he has come near to launching a female attack on his own misogyny. The poem is less a masculine manifesto than an unresolved argument.

'To My Wife', written early in 1951 shortly after Larkin had moved to Belfast, adopts an opposite rhetorical strategy to that in 'Deceptions'. Instead of taking the part of a rapist, the poet here imagines himself in the role of a husband. The result is equally uneasy:

> Simply to choose stopped all ways up but one,
> And sent the tease-birds from the bushes flapping.
> No future now. I and you now, alone.
>
> So for your face I have exchanged all faces,
> For your few properties bargained the brisk
> Baggage, the mask-and-magic-man's regalia.
> Now you become my boredom and my failure,
> Another way of suffering, a risk,
> A heavier-than-air hypostasis.
>
> (CP, 54)

Again an anxious subtext makes itself heard. The symbolist vagueness of the flapping 'tease-birds' and the tricksy Yeatsian glamour of 'the mask-and-magic-man's regalia' evocatively celebrate the life of aesthetic freedom. But the poet's tone seems unpleasantly ruthless beneath the polished phrases. It is disturbingly apparent that a score is being paid off against this 'wife'. There is a cruel animus in the meagre adjective 'few' ('your few properties'), contemptuously set against the rich and elaborate phrases which precede and follow it, describing the poet's imaginings. In the last two lines his poise falters. The phrasing becomes lumpy and the imagery ingeniously overtechnical: 'Another way of suffering, a risk,/ A heavier-than-air hypostasis'. Perhaps it was the disquieting element of personal malice in this poem which caused the poet to abandon it before it reached a finished enough state to publish.

As time passed, Larkin developed beyond the immediate pain of the crisis of 1950, though it still re-emerges here and there in wry retrospective reformulations. 'Letter to a Friend about Girls', completed in 1959, for example, shows a relaxed attempt to ironise the pattern of his own personal sexual history in terms of the comic categories of Amis's fiction. At last, Larkin confides, he has realised his friend's secret. They are, and always have been, on different planes of existence:

> After comparing lives with you for years
> I see how I've been losing: all the while
> I've met a different gauge of girl from yours . . .
> Before, I couldn't credit your intrigues
> Because I thought all girls the same, but yes,
> You bag real birds, though they're from alien covers.
>
> (*CP*, 122)

The poet goes on to summarise his friend's sex-life in a brilliant vignette of tacky sexual larks, such as those with which the Sunday newspapers excite the salacious envy of their readers:

> Now I believe your staggering skirmishes
> In train, tutorial and telephone booth,
> The wife whose husband watched away matches
> While she behaved so badly in a bath,
> And all the rest who beckon from that world
> Described on Sundays only, where to want
> Is straightway to be wanted, seek to find,
> And no one gets upset . . .
>
> (*CP*, 122)

Like the very different feminine myth of 'If, My Darling' this male myth of life as a promiscuous romp is grimly contrasted with the poet's 'realler' alternative. But again the contrast is not a simple one. After his unashamed envy of his friend's rakish exploits we expect him to invite a corresponding pity for himself because of the unglamourous 'gauge' of women to whose company he is condemned. But this is not quite what occurs. While the women in the first stanzas remain mere agents of male gratification, the poet's women insist on being more than mere agents of male frustration. They demand to be acknowledged and understood on their own terms:

> They have their world, not much compared with yours,
> But where they work, and age, and put off men
> By being unattractive, or too shy,
> Or having morals – anyhow, none give in:
> Some of them go quite rigid with disgust
> At anything but marriage: that's all lust
> And so not worth considering; they begin
> Fetching your hat, so that you have to lie
> Till everything's confused . . .
>
> (*CP*, 122–3)

Beneath the droll contrast between this friend's facile conquests and his own comic failures with women, the poet seems almost to be identifying himself with his particular 'gauge' of women, sympathising with them, and defending them from his friend's disregard. A faint note of moral earnestness even creeps in. And when the poet's irritation with their wrangling for a ring boils over, it is qualified by an exasperated admission of his own emotional involvement: 'you mine away/ For months, both of you, till the collapse comes/ Into remorse, tears, and wondering why/ You ever start such boring barren games.' Both he and the woman are in the same unhappy boat. Clearly this poet will never be able to see his women as birds to be bagged. That is the mere stuff of fantasy. His view of womankind is exasperatedly sympathetic rather than predatory. He and his friend play in 'separate leagues', and there is nothing he can do about it.

'Wild Oats', completed in 1962, dramatises a similar antithesis. Though the poet keeps the photographs of the 'bosomy English rose' as 'Unlucky charms', she was never destined for the likes of him. The 'friend in specs' to whom he writes 'over four hundred letters' during seven years, and yet whom he is too 'selfish' to marry, is more his 'gauge' of woman. But the neat sexual antithesis between the two women is again only the starting-point for the poem's meaning. The reductive phrases fail effectively to perform their sexual-political function in absolving him from his feelings of guilt and responsibility. The poem still echoes his vehement and bitter struggle to disengage himself from the responsibility of his engagement over a decade earlier: 'Further, women don't just sit still and back you up. They want children: they like scenes: they want a chance of parading all the emotional haberdashery they are stocked with. Above all they like feeling they "own" you – or that you "own" them – a thing I hate' (26.i.50). Far from 'sitting still' and answering the requirements of his male subjectivity, his fiancée in 'Wild Oats' actually imposes *her* subjectivity on the poet, reducing him to an object in her female domestic mythography. His sexist categories of 'bosomy rose' and 'friend in specs' yield to the feminine category of 'typically selfish' man. It is her tone of voice and her phrases which sound through his words:

> Parting, after about five
> Rehearsals, was an agreement
> That I was too selfish, withdrawn,
> And easily bored to love.
> Well, useful to get that learnt.
>
> (*CP*, 143)

But his surly tone shows him resentful of this image of himself which it seems he has accepted as the price of disentangling himself from the relationship. The oddly careful phrasing, 'Parting . . . was an agreement', is charged with irony, indicating his continuing unhappy protest against the lesson which she has made him learn. Pain and injured feelings still smoulder under the bleak finality of 'Well, useful to get that learnt'.

The more 'philosophical', or elegiac tone which Larkin adopts towards his own sexual history in such poems as 'Letter to a Friend' and 'Wild Oats' recurs in a more poised and assured form in several poems written at about the same time which deal with sexual stereotypes in a public rather than a personal context. Here Larkin moves beyond dramatised autobiography and attempts a more 'philosophical' analysis of the imaginative images of sex. 'The Large Cool Store' (*CP*, 135), 'Breadfruit' (*CP*, 141), 'Essential Beauty' (*CP*, 144), and 'Sunny Prestatyn' (*CP*, 149), all written in 1961–2 as Larkin approached 40, reflect with detached wit on male fantasies and female images. More profoundly they explore the gulf between the 'empirically true' and the banal myths by which we live. These poems are sometimes read as moral satires on false illusions. They are more truly seen as elegies on our pathetically impossible dreams of beauty and perfection. As Laurence Lerner says: 'Platonic beauty is a lie, as is the advertiser's patter; but without such lies, life would be boredom and fear' (121). Larkin seems, for instance, to be celebrating the naïve preposterousness of the advertising images in 'Essential Beauty' rather than seeking to replace their false images with some 'healthier' view of the world: 'High above the gutter/ A silver knife sinks into golden butter,/ A glass of milk stands in a meadow.' And the description of the dying smokers' vision of 'that unfocused she/ No match lit up, nor drag ever brought near,/ Who now stands newly clear,/ Smiling, and recognising, and going dark' (*CP*, 144–5) subsumes an attack on the use of sex in tobacco advertising into a bitter protest against the pain and anguish of death.

'Breadfruit' offers a most simple and engaging contrast of fantasy with reality, in the form of an updated anti-pastoral:

> Boys dream of native girls who bring breadfruit,
>   Whatever they are,
> As brides to teach them how to execute
> Sixteen sexual positions on the sand;
> This makes them join (the boys) the tennis club,
> Jive at the Mecca, use deodorants, and
> On Saturdays squire ex-schoolgirls to the pub
>   By private car.
>
>   (*CP*, 141)

The humour is merciless, and the male reader in particular is likely to wince as he laughs:

> Such uncorrected visions end in church
>   Or registrar:

A mortgaged semi- with a silver birch;
Nippers; the widowed mum; having to scheme
With money; illness; age. So absolute
Maturity falls, when old men sit and dream
Of naked native girls who bring breadfruit
   Whatever they are.

                        (*CP*, 141)

If 'Dry-Point' explored sex-as-biology this poem explores sex-as-socialised-romance. Both aspects of sex last as long as life itself. Though the absolutely mature old men know that docile and athletic native girls will, alas, never bring them the exotic, comically voluptuous breadfruit ('Whatever they are'), they still sit and dream. The version of 'real' married life in the final stanza perhaps risks descending into a kind of stand-up comedian's reduction of marriage to mothers-in-law and domestic discomforts. But characteristically Larkin transcends mere caricature by shifting in a few phrases from joky social comedy to bleak elegy: 'Nippers; the widowed mum; having to scheme/ With money; illness; age'. This poem could seem merely cynical, with its neatly circular form and its comic light-verse manner. But beneath its apparently reductive jeer at life's sordidness lies an elegy on the pathetic fantasies by which we live, and the inevitability of their disappointment.

'Sunny Prestatyn' offers a more complex treatment of the familiar sexual imagery of the advertising industry. Larkin describes the subject of the poem on the *Listen* record of *The Whitsun Weddings* as 'one of those jolly, colourful posters that are so beloved of publicity-officers of seaside towns, showing the universal symbol of happiness, a pretty girl'. On the surface level this is a social satire, the poet's elegant deconstruction of the sexual myth of the holiday poster closely resembling one of Roland Barthes' *Mythologies*. Like Barthes Larkin is impatient at the apparent 'naturalness' which the media and advertisers impart to ideologically loaded or commercially manipulative images (Barthes, 11). On this level the poem treats the way the image of the girl is used by the advertiser to overwhelm the viewer's senses, and dispel all contradictions in what Barthes would call the 'euphoric security' of myth:

   Come To Sunny Prestatyn
   Laughed the girl on the poster,

> Kneeling up on the sand
> In tautened white satin.
> Behind her, a hunk of coast, a
> Hotel with palms
> Seemed to expand from her thighs and
> Spread breast-lifting arms.
>
> (*CP*, 149)

Erotic implications are subtly manipulated by the poster's designer. The girl's body is elided with the landscape; and both are available (apparently) to the male holidaymaker. The coast over which he might ramble, the hotel in which he might stay, seem to 'expand from her thighs'. Even the grammar becomes confounded in the erotic tangle. At first sight it seems that the girl's raised arms simply serve to lift her breasts in innocent provocativeness, 'Spread' being an adjective modifying 'arms'. But in this case one would have expected a comma after 'Spread'. The absence of this comma suggests that 'Spread' may be a verb, implying an even more suggestively erotic relationship between the landscape and the girl's body. Is it perhaps the personified 'hunk of coast' ('hunk' bearing its colloquial masculine sense) and the 'Hotel with *palms*' (a wild pun?), who 'spread' *their* 'arms', by a trick of perspective, to lift the girl's breasts? Larkin's own reading of the lines on the *Listen* record allows the slightest pause after 'Spread', leaving the ambiguity unresolved.

The male viewer is thus intended to give his euphoric assent to the girl's 'natural' reality, and take his next holiday in Prestatyn. However, she remains Myth masquerading as Nature, and her contradictions will not be dispelled. The price her image pays for its sexual perfection is its sexual inaccessibility on the poster. She gestures invitingly, but cannot be reached. In the context of the world which surrounds the poster her perfection, apparently so real and natural, is profoundly provocative and frustrating. Indeed, on one level, it is the advertiser's intention to evoke this frustration. In this perspective the vandalism of the poster is to be seen as a primitive form of deconstructive art-criticism. The girl is a 'universal symbol', and Titch Thomas and his friends distrust 'universal symbols' as profoundly (if not so articulately) as Larkin himself. Despite its crudity there is a certain gratifying wit in the way their graffiti deny the apparently innocent perfection of the image:

> She was slapped up one day in March.
> A couple of weeks, and her face
> Was snaggle-toothed and boss-eyed . . .
> *(CP, 149)*

They go on to draw out the subtext of erotic blackmail which is carefully mystified in this apparently innocent 'universal symbol of happiness':

> Huge tits and a fissured crotch
> Were scored well in, and the space
> Between her legs held scrawls
> That set her fairly astride
> A tuberous cock and balls
>
> Autographed *Titch Thomas* . . .
> *(CP, 149)*

Thus they take their revenge on the inaccessible girl for taunting them with their inadequacy (Titch Thomas's name suggests a source for his insecurity in the size of his 'John Thomas' – penis).

But the vandals' apparent triumph over the girl is also of course an acknowledgement of the power which her image exerts over them. (Some advertisers have been known to monitor the sexual defacement of their posters in order to assess their impact.) Given the manner in which Larkin describes this vandalism the question inevitably arises as to how much power her image exercises over the poet himself. How far is he in fact a detached Barthesian analyst, calmly deconstructing the girl's mythic power? Is he not rather himself a vicarious vandal, enjoying the girl's defilement? Matt Simpson, for instance, feels that 'the poet, in the act of recording, discovers himself to be too intently voyeuristic, an accomplice' (178). Janice Rossen speculates similarly on 'how much complicity the poet shares in the act' (73). She cannot fully accept Terry Whalen's morally favourable view of the graffiti as a 'healthy rebellion' against the 'fraudulence' of advertising (Whalen, 43–4), arguing that Larkin 'seems to justify violence against women by suggesting that access to the woman is something men have been unfairly deprived of' (Rossen, 74). As she observes: 'the lust which drives men to deface a poster can also lead one to rape an actual woman' (75). Rossen and

Simpson identify a disturbing complexity in Larkin's tone, and it may be suspected that male readers will always find this poem easier to enjoy than female ones.

But Rossen is mistaken in seeing the girl as primarily a 'deep subconscious' projection of Larkin's own sexist mythology: 'As a siren, she drives men to commit bizarre and brutal acts . . . as a prostitute, according to this logic, she deserved the punishment anyway' (74–5). This is the 'logic' of Titch Thomas, not of Larkin. Larkin does share to some degree the violent impulses of his vandals, but he is also horrified by his own impulses. He said that the poem was intended to be 'horrific' as well as 'funny', and the horror of the poem comes precisely from his awareness of the dual nature of the image on the poster. The reader may feel moral satisfaction at the vandals' destruction of a fraudulent commercial image (Whalen), or immoral gratification at their revenge on unattainable womanhood (Rossen). But this gratification is qualified by the simple horror of watching the defilement of a 'pretty girl'. The shocking brutality of '*She* was slapped up' (rather than 'It was slapped up') does not merely express the poet's relish of vicarious violence. It is also a chilling reminder that ultimately the image, however ideologically determined, is that of a real girl in a real place, 'empirically true', and painfully vulnerable. Here Larkin's vision of the poster transcends ideological categories. The girl is ultimately neither the mythic siren to which the vandals respond, nor the prostitute-figure of sexist fantasy or puritan moralism. In the final analysis the poem is not a 'subconscious' expression of Larkin's own sexist ideology, nor a Barthesian deconstruction of male mythology, nor an 'angry' satire on advertising, though all these elements are present within it.

The key to the poem's effect lies in the virtuoso line: 'She was too good for this life'. Following the horror and brutal gusto of the previous passage this mock-heroic cliché is robbed of the comic irony one might have expected of it in this context. It becomes quietly dismissive, as though the destruction of the girl was too painful (and too inevitable) to dwell on. And beneath this dismissiveness lies a lament for the vulnerable transience of the beauty and happiness of which she is the symbol, a lament all the more poignant for its abject banality. Both Rossen and Whalen reduce the line to an ironic attack on the falsity of the girl's appeal. Simpson, with more complexity, feels that it is intended to sound 'embarrassed and feeble'. Otherwise, Simpson says, it must be 'a cop out', since the girl 'was only ever *in* this world vicariously through art' (179). But ultimately for Larkin the girl's appeal is not false, or only false because, as the final fate of the poster indicates, transience and disease always overtake youth and beauty. On this level the girl is no ideological construct. However vicarious her image is, it really does represent 'how life should be' (*CP*, 144), how we would all like it to be: youthful, innocent, relaxed, sexually unproblematic. Indeed it is this glimpse of unsullied happiness, rather than her sexuality, which perhaps constitutes her most unbearable provocation to the vandals. Ultimately, and crucially, Larkin does not follow Barthes in denying the existence of 'universal' truths, or a real 'unhistorical' nature. His girl really does represent a happiness immune to ideological deconstruction, vulnerable only to the unmediated blows of life itself. Social satire and sexual politics are transcended by sorrow at the triumph of sordid reality over beautiful dream.

It is significant here that the final destruction of this 'universal symbol of happiness' is not the work of sexually aggressive delinquents:

> She was too good for this life.
> Very soon, a great transverse tear
> Left only a hand and some blue.
> Now *Fight Cancer* is there.
>
> (*CP*, 149)

The actual, real girl whose image is displayed on the poster is, for all her mystified perfection, no more immune to (say) cancer than Titch Thomas, or Larkin, or for that matter the reader of the poem. Whalen detects an oblique satirical reference to the 'cancer' of advertising in the last line (44). Simpson sees it as 'an adolescent's rhetorical flourish' (179). But the catch in Larkin's voice as he reaches this word on the *Listen* recording conveys no hint of satire or of melodrama.

'The Large Cool Store' follows the same threefold pattern of thesis, antithesis, synthesis as is seen in 'Sunny Prestatyn'. But instead of setting beautiful dream against crude reality and ending with laconic bleakness, it moves in the opposite direction, ascending from drab reality, through the ideal escape world of sexy night-clothes, to a lyrically expansive meditation on our 'unreal fantasies':

The large cool store selling cheap clothes
Set out in simple sizes plainly
(Knitwear, Summer Casuals, Hose,
In browns and greys, maroon and navy)
Conjures up the weekday world . . .

But past the heaps of shirts and trousers
Spread the stands of Modes For Night:
Machine-embroidered, thin as blouses,

Lemon, sapphire, moss-green, rose
Bri-Nylon Baby-Dolls and Shorties
Flounce in clusters . . .

(CP, 135)

At first this seems mere versified sociology, as the poet muses on the way intimate erotic dreams are ruthlessly exposed in the market-place in mass-produced, 'machine-embroidered' form. There is something both comic and pathetic in the way the supposedly private 'secrets' of the bedroom are classified for public sale with the same matter-of-factness as the clothes of the 'weekday world': 'Knitwear, Summer Casuals, Hose . . . Bri-Nylon Baby-Dolls and Shorties'. Where the male shopper usually drops his eyes or casts a furtive, fascinated glance, the poet remains disconcertingly attentive to this social paradox.

It is the third stage of the poem, leading by a typical breath-drawing anticipatory enjambement into the final stanza ('shows// How . . .'), which unexpectedly develops from this embarrassing material one of those elevated reflective conclusions which characterise Larkin's most moving poems:

To suppose
They share that world, to think their sort is
Matched by something in it, shows

How separate and unearthly love is,
Or women are, or what they do,
Or in our young unreal wishes
Seem to be: synthetic, new,
And natureless in ecstasies.

(CP, 135)

The careful meditative intricacy of the syntax imparts a surprising gravity to the theme. There is a faltering hesitancy about the repeated infinitives in the two noun phrases ('To suppose . . . to think . . .') which form the elaborate subject of the sentence, governing the pivotal verb 'shows'. Moreover the grammatical objects which follow the verb also turn out to be puzzled and questing abstract noun clauses, returning us to the same meditative, pensive tone: 'How separate and unearthly love is,/ Or women are, or what they do,/ Or . . ./ Seem to be.'

Larkin remarks ruefully on the *Listen* record that one reviewer called 'The Large Cool Store' 'a silly poem about nighties'. But though the rhetoric of Larkin's poem may appear trivial and unpoetic compared with that of, say, 'Sailing to Byzantium', the difference is merely superficial. Indeed 'The Large Cool Store' is an essentially similar poem to Yeats's, and concerned with very much the same theme. Yeats's 'mythic', exotic image of a golden bird, 'set upon a golden bough to sing/ To lords and ladies of Byzantium', is every bit as 'silly' as a symbol of ideal perfection, as the social-realist 'baby-doll' nighties of the 1960s described by Larkin. And despite, or rather because of, their silliness, both images beautifully embody our yearning for an impossible world where the problems of 'Whatever is begotten, born, and dies', or 'the weekday world', are left behind.

Admittedly, there are major differences in rhetoric and imagery. Yeats's images are borrowed from the 'myth-kitty', Larkin's from everyday observation. But the similarities are equally striking, and go deeper. Both poets depict their ideal world in sensuously aesthetic terms of exotic colour and texture: 'hammered gold and gold enamelling'; 'Lemon, sapphire, moss-green, rose/ Bri-nylon'. In both poems it is the state of being outside nature, or 'natureless', which protects the ideal from the sordid muddle of reality. Yeats, with a loud magnificence which drowns out irony, anticipates his entry into 'the artifice of eternity': 'Once out of nature I shall never take/ My bodily form from any natural thing.' Larkin projects transcendence in terms of sexual fantasy: 'How separate and unearthly love is,/ Or women are, . . . synthetic, new,/ And natureless in ecstasies.' In both poems this 'natureless' ideal ultimately seems pathetically insubstantial and strained, leaving the reader at the end only with a more intensely poignant sense of inescapable reality.

LOVE

There remain those poems by Larkin featuring women, which neither reflect the sexual politics of his failed engagement nor ironise on the social iconography of sex. These are love poems, or poems about love, focusing on the five women (apart from his mother) to whom Larkin was closest: Monica Jones, Ruth Bowman, Winifred Arnott, Maeve Brennan, and the woman he addresses in 'When first we faced, and touching showed'. Some are private, informal poems like 'Long roots moor summer to our side of earth' (*CP*, 96), 'The Dance' (*CP*, 154–8), and 'Morning at last: there in the snow' (*CP*, 206), none of which was published until after Larkin's death. A few are elaborate set pieces, such as 'Lines on a Young Lady's Photograph Album' (*CP*, 71–2), and 'Maiden Name' (*CP*, 101). They express a surprisingly wide range of emotional nuances. Characteristically the poet addresses a woman, as in a conversation, with easy intimacy, evoking by implication the unique human context which they share. Even to a reader without knowledge of the biographical background, these poems at once reveal particular relationships at particular moments. Larkin's poetry of love is filled with real women in real places, and a sense of a shared humanity between the sexes. Like Hardy, Larkin leaves the reader with a sense of the discontinuous history of his affections, some of them simple and short-lived, some complex and lifelong.

The ease of address in Larkin's mature love poems was won only after a long literary (and emotional) apprenticeship. Earlier in his development he had adopted the different strategy of boldly identifying himself with a female centre of consciousness. At one point in *Jill* the elation of the 'rather feminine' protagonist is evoked through a startling female image: 'For one curious transient second he thought he knew how a bride feels on the morning of her wedding' (195). The reflections of Katherine in *A Girl in Winter* show an even more ambitious venture into female consciousness. The early poem, 'Wedding-Wind', completed in 1946 during the early stage of his relationship with Ruth Bowman, relies on a similar technique of dramatised empathy:

> Now in the day
> All's ravelled under the sun by the wind's blowing.
> He has gone to look at the floods, and I

Carry a chipped pail to the chicken-run,
Set it down, and stare. All is the wind
Hunting through clouds and forests, thrashing
My apron and the hanging cloths on the line.
Can it be borne, this bodying-forth by wind
Of joy my actions turn on, like a thread
Carrying beads?

(*CP*, 11)

Ignoring the risks, the youthful poet boldly adopts the voice of this farmer's wife. The result is somewhat artificial, recalling the midland pastoral atmosphere of early D. H. Lawrence, with added touches from Dylan Thomas. External images of nature are forced to do duty for internal emotional insights and, beautiful though it is in its way, it remains an accomplished exercise rather than a work of original inspiration.

As we have seen, in 'Deceptions', and other poems completed during and immediately after his engagement, this intimate identification with a female consciousness becomes complicated and spoiled by guilts and reproaches. It is only when Larkin steps back from commitment, after the move to Belfast in October 1950, that a new assured tone begins, tentatively, to emerge. 'Latest Face', completed in February 1951, shows the poet insistent in his rejection of domestic responsibility and guilt. It is the tenuous incipience of a possible relationship which he chooses to celebrate, rather than any actual human contact:

Admirer and admired embrace
On a useless level, where
I contain your current grace,
You my judgement; yet to move
Into real untidy air
Brings no lasting attribute –
Bargains, suffering, and love,
Not this always-planned salute.

(*CP*, 53)

The movement into 'real untidy air', the poet insists, would destroy both the 'vagrant' quality which is essential to the face's beauty and the uselessness which gives their 'embrace' its precious quality. The poem rejects both the ingenuous romanticism of 'Wedding-Wind' and the emotional guilt of 'Deceptions'. Aesthetics is preferred to emotion, and the delicate generosity of the poet's tone is made possible only by the lack of any real human commitment. The obscure last lines of the poem even seem to show the poet strategising his escape from any involvement which might threaten to develop.

But in the two poems addressed to Winifred Arnott, written shortly afterwards, the poet's traumatised anxiety is suddenly dispelled, and his imagination is released. 'Lines on a Young Lady's Photograph Album', completed in 1953, projects the relationship not in terms of the abstract aesthetic categories of 'admirer' and 'admired', but through playfully comic social stereotypes: the swivel-eyed lecher, the girl in pigtails or trilby hat. The poet's irresponsible sexuality is no longer the source of defensive guilt, as it was in 'Deceptions' and 'If, My Darling'. Here, in the context of this different relationship, it becomes a vehicle of flirtation:

> My swivel eye hungers from pose to pose –
> In pigtails, clutching a reluctant cat;
> Or furred yourself, a sweet girl-graduate;
> Or lifting a heavy-headed rose
> Beneath a trellis, or in a trilby hat
>
> (Faintly disturbing, that, in several ways) –
> From every side you strike at my control . . .
>
> (*CP*, 71)

The poet portrays himself in the stereotypical terms of a bachelor admirer, defenceless against the woman's charms. Significantly it is the girlish images of her youth that most strongly elicit his self-parodic lubricity, not her present self. Through his expressions of admiration for the girl in the photographs the speaker establishes a more complex, emotional relationship with the woman this girl has now become. He invites her to share his appreciation of her distant, younger selves, and in so doing, to acknowledge that she is growing older. The 'Faithful and disappointing' art of photography shows by its ingenuous preservation of vanished reality how irrevocable her past is:

> Those flowers, that gate,

> These misty parks and motors, lacerate
> Simply by being over; you
> Contract my heart by looking out of date.
>
> *(CP*, 72)

There is warm sympathetic affection here, beautifully enhanced by the absurd Cole Porter patness of the rhyme 'that gate/ lacerate'.

This poem is a most rare and unusual achievement. It has something of the quality of a verse epistle by Pope to Martha Blount – a mature delicate communication between grown-ups, worldly-wise and unillusioned, an expression of human solidarity and elegiac sympathy. There is an absence of any ulterior design on the part of the author:

> So I am left
> To mourn (without a chance of consequence)
> You, balanced on a bike against a fence;
> To wonder if you'd spot the theft
> Of this one of you bathing; to condense,
>
> In short, a past that no one now can share,
> No matter whose your future; calm and dry,
> It holds you like a heaven, and you lie
> Unvariably lovely there,
> Smaller and clearer as the years go by.
>
> *(CP*, 72)

The poet cannot now, alas, share her past. But he does share her sharp sense that it is past. There is no sense here, as there almost always is in poems addressed by men to real or imagined women, that he is trying to 'put one over' on her. If this is a seduction poem (a reworking of the *carpe diem* theme), it is one whose fellow-feeling with the beloved goes beyond the usual sexual politics. Indeed it deliberately lays them bare in the self-dramatised ironic stereotypes of 'nice girl' and 'dirty old man' (though Larkin was in fact just 31 at the time).

In 'Maiden Name', completed early in 1955, the woman's name, with its 'five light sounds', serves, like the photographs, as the key to

her lost younger self. Like a mourner ('since you're past and gone')
the poet treasures her memory:

> It means what we feel now about you then:
> How beautiful you were, and near, and young,
> So vivid, you might still be there among
> Those first few days, unfingermarked again.

The name preserves a fixed and unchangeable ideal woman who
cannot now be touched by time, and remains forever undepreciated
by the passing years:

> So your old name shelters our faithfulness,
> Instead of losing shape and meaning less
> With your depreciating luggage laden.
>
> (*CP*, 101)

The poet ingeniously celebrates the woman's unvariably lovely
identity, in the form of her maiden name. But this identity has
preserved its shape and meaning precisely because it is 'disused'. As
in the case of the image on the poster in 'Sunny Prestatyn' the price
paid for perfection is inaccessibility. All the poet's rhetorical
expressions of faithfulness to the woman's 'unfingermarked' identity
ultimately reveal themselves as transparently hopeless attempts to
evade the poignant fact that the woman herself, unlike the name, will
inevitably 'depreciate' as she gathers the 'luggage' of her developing
experience.

The elaborate compliment and warm protectiveness of 'Lines on a
Young Lady's Photograph Album' and 'Maiden Name' do not recur
in Larkin's poems addressed to other women. His vision of Maeve
Brennan in 'Broadcast', for instance, with her 'new, slightly-
outmoded shoes' (*CP*, 140), hints at a more clearsighted, perhaps
teasing affectionateness. 'Poem about Oxford' is different again.
Subscribed 'for Monica', and probably written in 1970, it has a light
and relaxed tone, born of common tastes and experiences. This is
Larkin's only significant poem in consistent anapaests, the comfortable sing-song rhythms of which he makes the vehicle of affection-
ate humour:

> Aside from more durable things,
> I'm glad you don't say you're from Girton,
> You'd sooner I wasn't at King's;
> To all that it meant – a full notecase,
> Dull Bodley, draught beer, and dark blue,
> And most often losing the Boat Race –
> You're added, as I am for you.
>
> (*CP*, 179)

The list of the shared 'furniture' of his and Monica Jones's lives (leaving aside the 'more durable things' as not to be spoken of) is moving in its provincial privateness, with the hint of rivalry with Cambridge, and references to the 'butterless' austerity of their long-gone Oxford, 'In the depths of the Second World War'.

'When first we faced, and touching showed', completed late in 1975 when Larkin was 53, recapitulates the theme of the gulf between dream and reality, but in the new and original context of a relationship formed late in life, after many others. The play of self-dramatisation and irony of the earlier poems is replaced here by lyric simplicity:

> When first we faced, and touching showed
> How well we knew the early moves,
> Behind the moonlight and the frost,
> The excitement and the gratitude,
> There stood how much our meeting owed
> To other meetings, other loves.
>
> (*CP*, 205)

As in 'Lines on a Young Lady's Photograph Album', the poet regrets that he cannot share his beloved's past, which 'Belonged to others'. But here, in the much longer time-perspective of this poem, it is more difficult to make this reflection into a bridge between them. The experience of life which the lovers reveal in their knowledge of 'the early moves' may facilitate their coming together, but it also bears painful witness to the length of their separate pasts. 'The decades of a different life/ That opened past your inch-close eyes/ Belonged to others, lavished, lost.' Their only strategy can be to forget, to live for the moment. In an original variation on the *carpe diem* theme they must take no thought – not for the morrow – but for yesterday. Only in this way can older lovers like themselves preserve the sense of the unique newness of their relationship:

> no cost,
> No past, no people else at all –
> Only what meeting made us feel,
> So new, and gentle-sharp, and strange.
>
> (*CP*, 205)

But this sense of newness is very fragile. The 'pain', as the poet admits, is still 'real'.

At the very end of his poetic career, in September 1979, Larkin completed the shocking 'love poem' 'Love Again', begun some time earlier. It begins with an appallingly frank expression of the feelings of sexual frustration at being abandoned in favour of another man:

> Love again: wanking at ten past three
> (Surely he's taken her home by now?),
> The bedroom hot as a bakery,
> The drink gone dead, without showing how
> To meet tomorrow, and afterwards . . .
>
> (*CP* 215)

As he forecast in 'Dry-Point' in 1950, the 'time-honoured irritant' of sex still has him on its treadmill, decades later, masturbating with 'the usual pain, like dysentery'. Once again his sexual activity has been reduced to a biological affair between himself and his own body. Like the end of 'Dry-Point' also, the end of this poem presents an image of escape, but now expressed in more human terms than the abstract 'padlocked cube of light' of his younger imagination. The older poet seeks imaginative release, more humbly, in tentative guesses at the harmony and fulfilment which others may have found, or which perhaps – had his own upbringing or early relationships been different – he might have found himself.

Significantly also this imagined hypothetical alternative to his own

failure calls on images derived from the tradition of poetry which at
the beginning of his career he had felt impelled to reject:

> but why put it into words?
> Isolate rather this element
>
> That spreads through other lives like a tree
> And sways them on in a sort of sense
> And say why it never worked for me.
> Something to do with violence
> A long way back, and wrong rewards,
> And arrogant eternity.
>
> (CP, 215)

At the beginning of his poetic career Larkin had abandoned the
metaphysical euphoria of Yeats. He rejected Yeats's heady rhetorical
elisions between subjective and objective, and his romantic celebration of life's multifaceted unity:

> O chestnut-tree, great-rooted blossomer,
> Are you the leaf, the blossom or the bole?
> O body swayed to music, O brightening glance,
> How can we know the dancer from the dance?
>
> ('Among School Children')

Larkin, as we have seen, was unable to 'jack [him]self up' to such
sacramental fervour. In his *Oxford Book of Twentieth Century English
Verse* he included a poem by Amis, in which the poet addresses a
young man lusting after the 'Forthcoming models' among the
schoolgirls passing by his window:

> You can't win, Dai. Nature's got all the cards.
> But bear up: you still know the bloody leaf
> From bole or blossom, dancer from the dance.
>   Hope for you yet, then.
>
> (OBTCEV, 532)

But here in his bedroom, 'hot as a bakery', the ageing Larkin no
longer shares Amis's cocky cynicism. He may not have been able to
jack himself up to it, but he nevertheless still hopelessly yearns after

'this element// That spreads through other lives like a tree/ And sways them on in a sort of sense', though he still knows that callous Nature has in fact 'got all the cards', and that the endless nothingness of 'arrogant eternity' dispels all Yeatsian dreams.

5

'Beyond all this'

DEATH, AGE, AND ABSENCE

DEATH

Poetic responses to death divide into two different, though not mutually exclusive, categories: the religious and the secular. On the one hand, poets like Donne and Tennyson offer the promise, or at least the hope, of 'eternal life' transcending death. On the other hand, poets like Arnold and Hardy seek merely to share their sorrow in the face of death's finality. In the eighteenth and nineteenth centuries, as religious belief waned, the religious and secular responses were often blended uneasily together. Gray, for example, expresses conventional belief in the afterlife, but is nevertheless far more concerned in his poetry with death as the end of existence than as a road to eternity. Larkin is more consistent, explicitly discounting religious belief. Death in his work prompts emotion rather than metaphysical or theological assertion. It gives him pause for thought rather than intimations of immortality. The church in 'Church Going' is a place 'proper to grow wise in,/ If only that so many dead lie round' (*CP*, 98). Despite the wishful thinking of some critics (Parkinson, 231) there is no religious content to this 'wisdom', and the phrasing ('If only . . .') is distinctly casual and concessive. Larkin denied that this poem, his most extended treatment of religion, was in any sense itself religious:

> It is of course an entirely secular poem. I was a bit irritated
> by an American who insisted to me it was a religious poem.
> It isn't religious at all. Religion surely means that the affairs
> of this world are under divine superveillance, and so on, and
> I go to some pains to point out that I don't bother about that
> kind of thing, that I'm deliberately ignorant of it – 'Up at
> the holy end', for instance. (in Hamilton, 73)

His values are of this world, not the next: 'The ultimate joy is to be
alive, in the flesh' (23.vi.41). In 'Aubade' he depicts religion as
simply a failed attempt to transcend death:

> This is a special way of being afraid
> No trick dispels. Religion used to try,
> That vast moth-eaten musical brocade
> Created to pretend we never die . . .
> > (*CP*, 208)

However, despite his dismissal of the large claims of religion,
Larkin remains a secular rather than an atheist poet. He is
unreligious rather than anti-religious. This is a crucial distinction
and essential to the universal appeal of his elegiac poems. He early
and completely lost the anti-Christian fervour with which he advised
Sutton to use Lawrentian 'Etruscan' iconography in his painting:
'No fucking Christianity' (16.xii.40). His mature poetry contains no
atheistic philosophisings like those in Hardy's 'Transformations' or
'Nature's Questioning'. Larkin has no anger against God for not
existing, nor does he generate the kind of atheistic spirituality found
in the works of A. E. Housman or Stevie Smith. Housman's atheism
can sound almost religious:

> From far, from eve and morning
> > And yon twelve-winded sky,
> The stuff of life to knit me
> > Blew hither: here am I.

Larkin, in contrast, is emotional rather than spiritual:

> At death, you break up: the bits that were you
> Start speeding away from each other for ever

With no one to see. It's only oblivion, true:
We had it before, but then it was going to end . . .

(CP, 196)

Though he admired Stevie Smith's writing, Larkin felt that her constant preoccupation with 'the concepts and language of Christianity' did not 'make the best poems', and accuses some of her work of 'a kind of Rationalist Press sunlessness (*RW*, 156–7). He is unwilling to limit the appeal of his work by picking quarrels with particular religious beliefs, or championing atheistic philosophy. He simply refuses to 'bother about that kind of thing'. Consequently religious beliefs arouse his compassion rather than his anger. Religion in his work is seen as another of the pathetic ideals by which we live, a beautiful but vain delusion. Time may have 'disproved' all the hopes of the moustached women in their frocks at the evangelical meeting in 'Faith Healing' (*CP*, 126). But the poem is not designed to demonstrate or prove any such clear-sighted intellectual judgement. The poem's focus falls rather on the ordinary emotional yearning for self-transcendence which the women's faith expresses:

What's wrong! Moustached in flowered frocks they shake:
By now, all's wrong. In everyone there sleeps
A sense of life lived according to love.
To some it means the difference they could make
By loving others, but across most it sweeps
As all they might have done had they been loved.
That nothing cures.

(CP, 126)

Illusory though it is, the women's substitution of divine love for the human love which they have missed is unbearably moving. This unembarrassed and unstrident atheism gives Larkin's treatment of death a simple unreligious universality.

On the literary level also Larkin carefully ensures the widest appeal for his elegies by establishing an uncontroversial middle-ground. His poems about death are, in the best sense of the word, conventional works. Death is after all the most familiar, even banal of topics. Too much display of brilliance or originality in treating it will almost inevitably seem in bad taste. Like many aspiring inexperienced poets the youthful Larkin saw in death a convenient universal theme on which to practise his craft. But right from the beginning he was acutely aware of the difficulty of writing distinctively on this subject without alienating the reader. In a letter written a month after his seventeenth birthday he confessed, with a self-criticism astonishing in one so young:

> I have just written a pretty ghastly poem starting:
> 'If this one night should lengthen into eternity
> And this innocent sleep deepen to death . . .'
> Full of gloom and adolescent self-conceit and windbag sentimentality and pseudo-Keatsian mush.
>
> (6.ix.39)

The pseudo-Keatsian 'mush' he was producing at the age of seventeen was followed by Yeatsian, Audenesque and Dylanesque exercises on the same subject. But even after Larkin had matured beyond simple imitation, his poems on death still, almost inevitably, possess a formal and tonal conventionality lacking in his poems on (say) women or ageing. They do not proclaim their originality, frequently presenting themselves as 'set-pieces' in established genres. Thus 'Going' is a gnomic riddle, 'An April Sunday brings the snow' a personal elegy, 'Next, Please' an extended conceit, 'An Arundel Tomb' an ironic ode on the familiar theme of the triumph of art over death. These poems on death show the poet applying his 'individual talent' to the 'tradition' in an unusually lucid and self-conscious way, generating unique 'freshly created universes' certainly – but out of the most familiar materials.

Larkin's first mature treatment of the subject is the polished literary exercise 'Going', probably completed in February 1946, whose teasing obliquity suggests a primitive Anglo-Saxon riddle. Its immediate model, however, is Imagism. The poem has all the Imagist mannerisms: confident brevity, symbolist imagery, abrupt sentences, varying line lengths, absence of rhyme and culminating rhetorical questions. Moreover the way the initial regular iambs collapse into virtual free verse at the end of the poem embodies, with the technical concentration of a true Poundian *image*, the sensation of fading consciousness. In one respect only does Larkin modify the Imagist prescription. Apart from the hanging last line, the stanzas are regular: tetrameter, pentameter, dimeter:

There is an evening coming in
Across the fields, one never seen before,
That lights no lamps.

Silken it seems at a distance, yet
When it is drawn up over the knees and breast
It brings no comfort.

Where has the tree gone, that locked
Earth to the sky? What is under my hands,
That I cannot feel?

What loads my hands down?

(CP, 3)

The Imagist mannerisms offer the poet none of the false security of
the Yeatsian rhetoric which he generally preferred at this time. He is
compelled to overcome some technical resistance, and consequently
the poem never mistakes itself, as many of his other early imitative
poems do, for anything more than a coolly playful genre-piece. Still
bewitched by Yeats, however, Larkin seems not at first to have
realised that he had written a finer work than such a self-conscious
literary exercise ought to be. Originally he gave it the jokily punning
title 'Dying Day', only later changing this to 'Going', which though
equally teasing, implies more gravity.

Two years later, in 1948, Larkin produced his first major elegiac
poem, 'An April Sunday brings the snow', the only poem in his
oeuvre which takes the form of an elegy for an actual loved person.
Here the literary allegiances are less specific. The poem has the
informally meditative tone common to much elegiac verse from
Shakespeare's sonnets to Edward Thomas, while the imagery seems
quite spontaneous – but nevertheless also familiar. The effect is
characteristically conventional and at the same time effortlessly
original:

An April Sunday brings the snow
Making the blossom on the plum trees green,
Not white . . .

(CP, 21)

The casual conversational tone, and the poet's concern to be accurate

139

about the visual effect which has surprised him, establish an unsymbolic, irreducible reality. It is important to the impact of the poem that the reader should not doubt that the poet's attention was actually caught from the kitchen window by this peculiar effect of the light. His observation is no second-hand literary trope. But despite its undoubted contingent authenticity, it *is* of course a literary trope, frost on flowers having been a conventional image of untimely death since the Middle Ages. Larkin's particular variation, however – snow on plum-blossom – still carries a non-literary conviction; and the authenticity of the poem is paradoxically reinforced rather than shaken by the recognition of the literary precedents. The poet's emotion expresses itself quite naturally in familiar artifice.

The intimately moving ending of the poem again unites an authentic 'here and now' with a conventional elegiac trope. The poet is moving from cupboard to cupboard with 'five loads' of jam made by his father from the fruit of the same trees whose blossom is now covered in snow:

> More than enough for all next summer's teas,
>
> Which now you will not sit and eat.
> Behind the glass, under the cellophane,
> Remains your final summer – sweet
> And meaningless, and not to come again.
>
> (*CP*, 21)

The homely reference to 'next summer's teas', and the unforced use of the modern commercial word 'cellophane', imply an irreducible, non-metaphoric reality, made philosophically explicit in the sceptical verdict 'meaningless'. Moreover, the offhand collocation 'sweet/ And meaningless', is strangely resonant in its delicate metonymic identification of his father's life with the jam he has left behind. The self-evident, almost tautological meaninglessness of the jam (how can jam have 'meaning'?) is delicately transferred through the shared adjective 'sweet' to his father's 'last summer', which after his death has no other 'meaning' than the jam. But once again, for all its unique specificity, even gaucheness, the poem's rhetoric at this point is a familiar one. The jam has the same pathos as the burnt grass in 'Where the Picnic Was' by Thomas Hardy. It offers a heart-chilling reminder that the person who gave meaning to the thing has gone, while the thing itself remains. The effect is intensified by the poet's apparently incidental reference to the quantity of the jam. His odd hint of gratitude (or is it perhaps irritation?) that his father has made 'More than enough' develops into a vista of the future teas at which the jam will remind those who consume it of its maker's absence. The force of loss is conveyed by evoking the undisturbed course of the life from which the dead person has departed. And by the same moving illogicality with which Hardy in 'The Walk' tells the dead Emma that he has travelled their familiar route without her, Larkin here tells his dead father that he will not 'now' eat the jam he has made.

'Next, Please', completed early in 1951, offers a strong contrast of genre, being public and sententious, rather than private and lyrical. With truly Elizabethan gusto it elaborates the riddling effect of 'Going' into an inflated conceit, based on the proverbial ship that we are all waiting 'to come in'. But the tawdry, unreal glamour of Larkin's ships breathes new life into the dead metaphor and gives a wry irony to the Elizabethan resonance of the poem. His 'armada of promises', in a brilliantly original touch, translates the full-riggers of some inauthentic Hollywood period-romance into ominous symbolist abstractions:

> for, though nothing balks
> Each big approach, leaning with brasswork prinked,
> Each rope distinct,
>
> Flagged, and the figurehead with golden tits
> Arching our way, it never anchors . . .
>
> (CP, 52)

The wittily ingenious stanza-form also plays an entertaining part in the effect: the first two lines forming a pentameter couplet, which is followed by another couplet the second line of which is curtailed to two feet, bringing the rhyme unexpectedly early. This shorter line is regularly enjambed into the following stanza, making for a little jauntily lugubrious anacrusis before the next disappointment comes along:

<pre>
                                                it's
No sooner present than it turns to past.
Right to the last
</pre>

We think each one will heave to and unload
All good into our lives, all we are owed
For waiting so devoutly and so long.
But we are wrong:

Only one ship is seeking us, a black-
Sailed unfamiliar, towing at her back
A huge and birdless silence. In her wake
No waters breed or break.

(CP, 52)

The abruptness of the last short line (which being final cannot be enjambed) curtly mimes the final disappointment of death. The rhymes are also neatly calculated: long vowels for the reflective opening ('we/ expectancy', 'day/ say', 'clear/ near'); brutal short syllables for the cruelly disappointing promise of the garish ships ('prinked/ distinct', 'tits/ it's'); lengthening out again towards the end ('past/ last', 'unload/ owed', 'long/ wrong'). The clever mechanics of the stanza-form in this poem, together with its elaborated metaphor, recall the intellectual wit of the Elizabethans and poets of the seventeenth century. And part of the strange exhilaration of the poem derives from the sophisticated freedom with which it combines its far-flung literary and cultural allusions.

Seldom again does Larkin aim at the extended conceit of 'Next, Please' in his treatment of death. Nevertheless, he frequently employs a similar wit in smaller-scale aphorisms. Death remains one of the great traditional subjects for the exercise of serious or comic wit, as the popularity of both strands of the epitaph genre shows. The severe economy of the epigram or aphorism, which frequently condemns it to mere triviality, becomes particularly effective and resonant when applied to the banal universality of death. Larkin never tired of composing epigrams on this simple but compulsive subject: 'Give me your arm, old toad;/ Help me down Cemetery Road' (CP, 148), 'And age, and then the only end of age' (CP, 153), 'nothing contravenes/ The coming dark' (CP, 193). The late poem 'Aubade', completed in 1977, offers a miniature anthology of such memorable aphorisms: 'Not to be here,/ Not to be anywhere,/

142

And soon', 'Most things may never happen: this one will', 'Being brave/ Lets no one off the grave', 'Death is no different whined at than withstood' (*CP*, 208–9).

'An Arundel Tomb', completed in February 1956, is (apart from 'The Building') Larkin's most extended and resonant set-piece on death. On one level it is a variant on the 'graveyard musing' which became popular in the eighteenth century: Larkin's equivalent of Gray's 'Elegy Written in a Country Churchyard' or Hardy's 'During Wind and Rain'. Its approach, however, is more philosophically adventurous than those of the conventionally pious Gray or the bleakly atheistic Hardy. It focuses, like Keats's 'Ode on a Grecian Urn' and Yeats's 'Sailing to Byzantium', on the transcendence of death through the one possible means open to the secular poet: art. Keats strives to affirm that the lovers' passion survives in the 'Cold Pastoral' of the urn, 'more happy' than in their lives. Yeats asserts that once 'out of nature', he will be immune to mortality, a golden bird upon a bough. Larkin explores our 'almost-instinct' that the love of the medieval couple still 'survives' in the sculptor's stone memorial. In fact none of these poets ultimately persuades himself of the reality of such transcendence. Their rhetorical straining after permanence reveals itself at the ends of their poems as an emotional strategy, an intense and moving form of pathetic fallacy: the imputing of human sympathies to emotionless nature, or in this case, art.

The first lines are casual and dispassionate, the desultory observations of a sightseeing tourist. They seem authentically 'natural', giving no hint of the literary and philosophical complexities to follow. The clasped hands of the statues take the poet by surprise: 'One sees, with a sharp tender shock,/ His hand withdrawn, holding her hand' (*CP*, 110). The casualness drops away. The aspirated h-alliteration sighs. The metre stammers with reversed feet

$$/ \quad x \qquad / \quad x \quad / \quad x$$
His hand . . . holding her hand . . .

The stress placed on 'His' and 'her' unites the figures in the verse, as they are united in the effigies, by a contradiction of conventional artistic decorum. But after this brief discomposure, the poet quickly regains his detachment, reflecting, with well-informed historical perspective, that the pre-baroque artist could not possibly have intended the apparent transcendence which he has accidentally achieved. The vivid human touch was merely a 'sculptor's . . . grace', added to help fix the onlooker's mind on what was really important to medieval eyes: 'The Latin names around the base'.

But the poet's subjective desire to find comfort in this icon of affection will not be reasoned away. His musing becomes more intense, even strenuous. The grammatical dislocation of stanza four, for instance, awkwardly enacts the discontinuity between the couple's medieval world and ours:

> They would not guess how early in
> Their supine stationary voyage
> The air would change to soundless damage,
> Turn the old tenantry away;
> How soon succeeding eyes begin
> To look, not read.

> (*CP*, 110)

The poet is caught ambiguously between two grammars. The sentence can be read 'correctly' as an unbroken sequence, establishing a continuity between the couple's world and ours: 'They would not guess how early . . ./ The air would change . . . [would]/ Turn the old tenantry away;/ [They would not guess] How soon succeeding eyes [would] begin/ To look, not read.' But the grammatical ellipses and the sheer clumsiness of these conditionals-within-a-conditional ('They *would* not guess how . . ./ The air *would*', etc.) makes it difficult for the reader to connect the later verbs in the sentence with the 'woulds' in the earlier part. It becomes tempting to break through the confusion by halting at the semi-colon, and reading 'How soon succeeding eyes . . .' as an exclamation on the part of the poet rather than a grammatical continuation of the sentence. This disjunction has the effect of converting 'begin' from a conditional to an indicative ('begin' rather than 'would begin'). It is as though the subject of the sentence changes as it progresses. We begin the stanza in the minds of the medieval couple, looking forward to an unknown hypothetical future when the air '*would* change', and – eventually – eyes 'would begin' to look rather than read. By the end of the stanza, their grammar of conditional futurity has been lost in a modern indicative present. Succeeding eyes now simply '*begin*/ To look, not read'.

This sense of the slippage of time, thus integrally worked into the language of the poem, both intensifies and undermines the poet's response to the frozen gesture of the hands. He is unable to deceive himself, romantically, that the long-dead medieval couple live on in stone. But he still, almost perversely, seeks consolation in the fact that they, or rather their effigies, have 'persisted'. In this sense at least, he insists, they have transcended death:

> Rigidly they
>
> Persisted, linked, through lengths and breadths
> Of time. Snow fell, undated. Light
> Each summer thronged the glass. A bright
> Litter of birdcalls strewed the same
> Bone-riddled ground. And up the paths
> The endless altered people came,
>
> Washing at their identity.
>
> (*CP*, 110–11)

But it is an unconvincing transcendence. The fleeting flux of the living world overwhelms the effigies with movement and colour. The poet depicts transience in rich and strange rhetoric, while the permanence of the rigid work of art remains bloodless and immobile. The innumerable repeated seasons flash by in no particular order: winter snow followed by the light of summer and the bright birdcalls of spring. The phrase 'Snow fell, undated' (when is snow ever dated?) evokes repeated obliterations. 'Light/ . . . thronged the glass' economically suggests the repeated growing and fading of light through a stained-glass window. 'A bright/ Litter of birdcalls' focuses a complex of semantic and grammatical ambiguities. 'A bright/ Litter' suggests 'brightly lit' (connected by internal rhyme with the 'light' thronging the glass); 'litter' suggests 'glitter'; the collocation of 'litter' and 'strewed' suggests casually disregarded debris. Possibly 'litter' also – very loosely – suggests that the birdcalls come from a brood of young. Moreover 'A bright/ Litter of birdcalls strewed . . .' is synaesthetic, metaphorically expressing something heard ('bright . . . birdcalls') in terms of something seen ('bright/ Litter . . . strewed'). The phrase beautifully evokes the profligacy of life as sensuous process: what Yeats calls 'Those dying generations'. In Larkin's version they become 'the endless altered

145

people', who, converted by yet another boldly implied metaphor into a rising tide, 'wash' at the medieval couple's identity.

The earl and countess have 'persisted' only to suffer humiliation, 'helpless' in the face of our neglect. The 'skeins' of smoke suspended over what is now merely their 'scrap' of history hint at air pollution and slow destruction. Like the jam which Larkin's father made, their effigies – sweet and meaningless (since only life – 'in the flesh' – has meaning) – survive merely to make more cruelly apparent the fact that they are dead and forgotten:

> Time has transfigured them into
> Untruth. The stone fidelity
> They hardly meant has come to be
> Their final blazon, and to prove
> Our almost-instinct almost true:
> What will survive of us is love.
>
> (*CP*, 111)

The sleight of hand whereby the final line *appears* to be a celebration of the transcendence which the whole sentence denies is pathetically ineffective. It is as far as the poet can honestly go.

The pathos of this tenuous ending is paradoxically only further intensified by the fact that Larkin has misdated the effigies, and more particularly their 'attitude' of clasped hands. By a delightful irony, the tomb in Chichester Cathedral which inspired the poem is not in fact pre-baroque, but a comprehensively reworked Victorian version by the sculptor Edward Richardson (1812–69). The original effigies, which presumably (but not certainly) depicted a fourteenth-century Earl of Arundel and his wife, had been defaced centuries before, during the Reformation and the Civil War. When Richardson started his work in the 1840s the original mutilated figures had become separated, the knight had no arms below his shoulders and the lady's right hand was missing. It was even uncertain on which side of her husband she had originally lain, and it was Richardson's decision to place her to the knight's right with her right hand held in his. Though the holding of hands is not unknown on original monuments a medieval knight would more usually have his hands pressed together in prayer (Foster *et al.*, 14–22). Moreover, the consolatory expressiveness of the hands in Richardson's version, not flatly palm to palm, but with her hand, fingers limply bent, resting in his large male palm, seems distinctly Victorian in spirit rather than medieval. In the *Monitor* television programme of 1964 Larkin expressed wry amusement at the unintended anachronisms in his poem. And indeed they can only serve to intensify its emotional effect, adding an additional poignant twist to the 'Untruth' into which the couple have been transfigured by Time, and by Time's mundane accomplice, the well-intentioned Victorian restorer. The couple could indeed hardly have meant the 'stone fidelity' of an 'attitude' which was almost certainly added to their effigies some four hundred years after their burial.

Larkin's elegiac poems characteristically focus on such images of failed transcendence: the 'disproved' faith of the women in 'Faith Healing', the jam which meaninglessly outlasts its maker, the 'stone fidelity' of the earl's and countess's clasped hands. 'The Building', completed in 1972, is a bleak later variant on the pattern, moving from the traditional elegiac locations of domestic interior and church to the world of modern amenities, hospitals and ambulances. It begins with a more elaborate and generalised version of the meditation of 'An Arundel Tomb': prompted not by the homely gesture of a religious monument, but by the intimidating grandeur of modern secular architecture. The hospital rises 'Higher than the handsomest hotel', though the poet seems uncertain whether its grand gesture is heroic or mock-heroic:

> The lucent comb shows up for miles, but see,
> All round it close-ribbed streets rise and fall
> Like a great sigh out of the last century.
> The porters are scruffy; what keep drawing up
> At the entrance are not taxis; and in the hall
> As well as creepers hangs a frightening smell.
>
> (*CP*, 191)

The tone is mixed and uneasy, ranging from initial eloquence to the final joky zeugma ('creepers' and 'smell' both 'hanging').

The middle stanzas of the poem develop this uneasiness, superstitiously avoiding the word 'hospital' (as the word 'ambulance' was avoided at the beginning, as though this poem was another riddle, like 'Going' or 'Next, Please' – thoug'. a feebler one. This slight obliquity lends a symbolic sinisterness to the building's 'rooms, and rooms past those,/ And more rooms yet, each one further off// And harder to return from'. Outside the gate of the hospital the poet has noticed a rival gesture of architectural transcendence, 'a locked church', forgotten among the traffic and the playing 'kids'. The contrast only serves to show more clearly that neither religion nor medicine can 'outbuild' death:

> That is what it means,
> This clean-sliced cliff; a struggle to transcend
> The thought of dying, for unless its powers
> Outbuild cathedrals nothing contravenes
> The coming dark, though crowds each evening try
>
> With wasteful, weak, propitiatory flowers.
>
> (*CP*, 192–3)

After the awesome architectural impersonality of the building, the flowers of the hospital visitors represent an altogether more intimate and human attempt to fend off the coming dark. But it is also a ridiculously feeble one. The isolated last line sounds almost like an afterthought, the sentence being grammatically complete at 'try', and the sadness of its tone is almost exasperatedly dismissive, with its sequence of three adjectives. The effect is clumsy, but carefully calculated. The suggestion of prudential common sense in 'wasteful . . .' is at once overwhelmed by the absurd tautology of 'weak . . . flowers'. Impossibly great demands are being made of them by the vain hopes of the visitors. Then the exhausted metrical stumbling of

$$x \quad / \ (x) \ x \ / \ x$$
prop i ti atory

reminds us that no god of suffering can in fact be appeased by such offerings. Finally the weight of this cruelly emphatic accumulation of epithets falls with crushing pathos on the soft consonants and open vowels of 'flowers'.

AGE

Larkin's poems concerning age are more original than those concerning death. No other major poet has devoted so much imaginative energy to the humiliations of ageing, to jealousy of the young and horror at approaching senility. 'Next, Please', 'An Arundel Tomb' and 'The Building' meditate on death as a fact or a state. Throughout his career, however, Larkin also wrote poems concerned with death as process, or rather with life as 'slow dying' (*CP*, 138). These poems on ageing adopt more intimately personal tones and, as Larkin grows older, they develop their own original rhetorical strategies. Frequently their literary manners are not so good as those of the more conventional elegies on death. Instead of eloquent resignation and muted sorrow we often find sardonic self-derision or angry humiliation. The poet still seeks and sometimes achieves elegiac detachment, but his rhetoric is bleaker, less warmly human than that in the more conventional elegies on death. These poems form a continuous series through the poet's career, developing and deepening over time. They fall into three broad phases. The earlier poems philosophise ironically over the sense of lost opportunities which comes with age. Then in the later 1960s, as he approaches 50, his philosophical composure cracks and he begins to express a raw jealousy of the young. Finally in the early 1970s he turns his attention in two highly original poems to the prospect of physical and mental senility.

The first poem in the series is the (presumably unfinished) 'Maturity', written in 1951, as Larkin approached the age of 30 (*CP*, 62). In an intimate tone, which scarcely seems directed at an audience, the poet reflects, with surprise, that he must already be in '*the prime of life*', a state which will last 'till my single body grows/ Inaccurate, tired . . .'. There is an undramatic humility about this comfortless prophecy which is distinctively 'Larkinesque'. It could be seen as the other, paradoxical side of that aggressively sure sense of himself seen in such poems as 'Self's the Man' (*CP*, 117) and 'Love' (*CP*, 150). This humility is again present in 'Skin', completed in April 1954 when Larkin was 31, but here it finds more engaging expression in light, whimsical wit. The poet apologises good-humouredly to his 'Obedient daily dress', which, as he grows older, 'must learn [its] lines':

> And pardon me, that I
> Could find, when you were new,
> No brash festivity
> To wear you at, such as
> Clothes are entitled to

Till the fashion changes.

(*CP*, 92)

The reference to death as a change of skin-fashion is playfully ingenious, with something of the riddling quality of 'Going' or 'Days'. But the poet's submissive acceptance of his past failures carries a bleak undertone. 'Triple Time' (*CP*, 73), in contrast, shows a more edgy wit, deriding 'our' myth of lost opportunities as a pathetic figment: 'the past,/ A valley cropped by fat neglected chances/ That we insensately forbore to fleece'. The humorous echo of the colloquial phrase 'fat chance' (i.e. 'no chance') has a caustic irony about it.

At this stage in his development the process of ageing still presents itself primarily in terms of a wasted past, or of lost opportunities. A particularly sustained and eloquent treatment of the theme is 'Reference Back', completed in 1955:

> Truly, though our element is time,
> We are not suited to the long perspectives
> Open at each instant of our lives.
> They link us to our losses: worse,
> They show us what we have as it once was,
> Blindingly undiminished, just as though
> By acting differently we could have kept it so.
>
> (*CP*, 106)

The deceptiveness of the dispassionately reasonable tone is revealed when this sententious, faintly stilted address to the reader is suddenly broken by the romantic excessiveness of 'Blindingly'.

All these early poems offer, with whatever ironies, a view of the ageing process as one of growing insight, 'The Coming of Wisdom with Time', as Yeats would have put it. They affect a dignified or at least a rueful resignation to the inevitable. 'Send No Money', however, completed in 1962, strikes a new and different note, abandoning philosophic calm for angry complaints expressed in Larkin's demotic register. There is something unsettlingly personal about the poet's sense of grievance in this poem, and it is presumably no coincidence that it was completed in the month of Larkin's fortieth birthday, August 1962. It is not always easy to make out the poet's intentions; both his tone and expression seem distorted by resentment. The title, for instance, refers obliquely to those discreet advertisements headed 'Send No Money', familiar in newspapers of the 1950s and 60s, in which catalogues of embarrassing items such as hernia trusses would be offered on credit. With barely controlled violence, the poet derides his dedication to the artistic quest for truth:

> Standing under the fobbed
> Impendent belly of Time
> *Tell me the truth*, I said,
> *Teach me the way things go.*
> All the other lads there
> Were itching to have a bash,
> But I thought wanting unfair:
> It and finding out clash.
>
> (*CP*, 146)

Time, personified as a pompous Dickensian patriarch (*Boy,/ There's no green in your eye . . .*'), grants the young poet his wish for clarity of vision at the cost of detachment from life. The grotesque oddity of the personification has the effect of an exasperated jibe, and the reported phrases project a strident irony not commensurate with any visible cause of offence. Significantly, on the *Listen* recording, though Larkin's reading is in general deceptively smooth, he seems to experience more difficulty than usual in controlling his stammer in these first lines. The reader experiences the odd embarrassment of suspecting that the poet may be 'losing his cool':

> *Oh, thank you*, I said, *Oh yes please*,
> And sat down to wait.
>
> Half life is over now,
> And I meet full face on dark mornings
> The bestial visor, bent in
> By the blows of what happened to happen.
> What does it prove? Sod all.
> In this way I spent youth,
> Tracing the trite untransferable
> Truss-advertisement, truth.
>
> (*CP*, 146)

151

He has sent no money, his credit has run out, and payment is now being exacted. The sight of his own ageing face in the mirror prompts the poet no longer to polite apologies to his dutiful skin, but to a barely articulate self-disgust, expressed in 'bad language' and vehemently crude alliterations. The knowledge of the truth which he has patiently gathered has brought no real wisdom. And in any case, like a truss-advertisement, it possesses after all no real glamour or mystery. It is merely 'trite'. And what is worst of all, his youth has been wasted in this useless quest.

Alongside the excessive, almost confessional rhetoric of this poem, Larkin develops in the early 1960s a new, harder, more chastened version of the composed reflective register heard in 'Reference Back'. In 'Dockery and Son', completed seven months after 'Send No Money' in March 1963, the poet regains his philosophical poise, but only to deliver a verdict of withering comfortlessness:

> Life is first boredom, then fear.
> Whether or not we use it, it goes,
> And leaves what something hidden from us chose,
> And age, and then the only end of age.
>
> (*CP*, 153)

Though Larkin's vocabulary of sex is quite explicit, death is not infrequently accorded the figleaf of a euphemism, as here, as though the poet's fear made him superstitious about naming the terrifying thing. However, the evasion is merely a gesture. Indeed the euphemism intensifies rather than muffles the dominant tone of appalling frankness. There is a disconcerting quality about such absolute cynicism.

This new grimness of tone was followed later in the 1960s by a shift in thematic focus from lost opportunities to lost youth. Larkin bids a bitter farewell to his own youth in 'The Dance', written in 1963-4, portraying his forty-year-old excitement as he exchanges glances with a woman at a dance: 'How useless to invite/ The sickened breathlessness of being young// Into my life again!' (*CP*, 157). But it is the unspent youth of others which begins to preoccupy him in the later 1960s. In such poems as 'High Windows' and 'Annus Mirabilis', both completed in 1967, he gives uninhibited expression, bitterly resigned or wittily comic, to this hopeless jealousy of those who are still young, and whose opportunities have yet to be lost. He is no longer concerned with 'fat neglected chances'. He does not regret having failed to take any particular opportunity himself, nor does he lament the wrong choices of his life. He simply regrets not being young. The 'paradise/ Everyone old has dreamed of' is always by definition the property of 'a couple of kids' (*CP*, 165). It can never again be his as it once was or, at least seemed to be in the eyes of an earlier generation of jealous adults. Similarly, the moment in 1963 when 'life was never better' came, unfortunately, 'just too late for me'. The 'Everyone' who in that year, 'Between the end of the *Chatterley* ban/ And the Beatles' first LP', suddenly began to feel that life was 'A quite unlosable game' cannot, in the very order of things, include the poet himself (*CP*, 167).

It is 'Sad Steps', completed in 1968, which gives the most poignant and vivid expression to this yearning for lost youth. Again, like the more conventional elegies, it is rich in literary echoes. But here the function of the allusions is more original and idiosyncratic. The confident gestures of previous writers on the familiar poetic subject of the moon provide an ironic intertext to his own jaded reflections, and the poem's restless, shifting register and second-hand imagery directly mirror the poet's listlessness. The title ironically recalls the thirty-first sonnet in Sir Philip Sidney's *Astrophel and Stella*: 'With how sad steps, O Moon, thou climbst the skies!' The sad steps which open Larkin's poem, however, are not those of an Elizabethan moon climbing the skies, but of the modern poet himself groping his way back to bed 'after a piss'. He is 'startled' by the beauty of the moonlit nightscape through the window, and is gripped by an unsettling euphoria. Disconcerted, he is unsure how to respond to this epiphany:

> There's something laughable about this,
>
> The way the moon dashes through clouds that blow
> Loosely as cannon-smoke to stand apart
> (Stone-coloured light sharpening the roofs below) . . .
> (CP, 169)

A laughably naïve (Elizabethan?) zest infuses the imagery, with its mock-heroic 'cannon-smoke', and the zeugma of the 'stone-coloured' light acting as a metaphorical whetstone 'sharpening' (the outline of) the roofs. The effect is not purely subjective and emotional, however. The self-conscious literariness of the imagery also accurately catches the strange stagey appearance of deserted moonlit gardens.

The Elizabethan poet had found an easy human solidarity with his moon, presuming by an artificial pathetic fallacy that its sadness was, like his own, the result of disappointment in love. Larkin's moon resists any such ingenuous literary rhetoric, and no gratifying conceit playfully identifies him with it. Nevertheless he makes the attempt to rise to the occasion and modulate into a sublimity worthy of this classic poetic subject:

> High and preposterous and separate –
> Lozenge of love! Medallion of art!
> O wolves of memory! Immensements! No,
>
> One shivers slightly, looking up there.
>
> (*CP*, 169)

His version, however, comes out neither as elegant conceit nor as sublime symbol, but as a grotesque parody of literariness, inflated and bombastic: 'Lozenge of love! Medallion of art!'. The extravagant coinage 'Immensements!', with its hint of Keatsian 'mush', is a gauche ultra-poeticism not to be found in the *Oxford English Dictionary*, nor in the 1987 *Supplement*. Such grandiosity is wryly deflated by a descent into the register of social chat: 'No,// One shivers slightly . . .'. Nevertheless the moon is on one level still performing its traditional poetic function, as a symbol of unattainable purity and hopeless passion:

> The hardness and the brightness and the plain
> Far-reaching singleness of that wide stare
>
> Is a reminder of the strength and pain
> Of being young; that it can't come again,
> But is for others undiminished somewhere.
>
> (*CP*, 169)

The ending of the poem opens out rhetorically, like those of 'At Grass', 'Ambulances', or 'Reference Back'. But a hint of desperation movingly flattens the effect. The rhythmic falling off of the last line, with its final reversed, falling foot –

154

/   x
somewhere

makes his resignation hopeless rather than consolatory, and the poem ends in a tone of humble abjection. The fact that others are still strong and young is apparently offered as a selfless palliation of the poet's pain. On the personal level however it is clearly the final twist of an envious knife. Perhaps this work, more than any other in Larkin's *œuvre*, bears out his paradox that 'A good poem about failure is a success' (*RW*, 74). The negativity of the work may be unremitting, but the writing is nevertheless exhilarating in its strange inventiveness.

In the early 1970s Larkin's tendency towards a kind of virtuoso self-parody intensified. 'The View', the poem with which he marked his fiftieth birthday in 1972, is a kind of quintessence of the casual self-deprecating wit of 'Skin' or 'Annus Mirabilis'. Its central image is from mountaineering, an incongruous choice for an ageing librarian, as he himself points out:

> The view is fine from fifty,
>   Experienced climbers say;
> So, overweight and shifty,
>   I turn to face the way
>   That led me to this day.

The stanza-form with its succession of five regular trimeters makes for a sardonic cheeriness, while the first ('a') rhyme is comically doubled, and increases in absurdity through the three stanzas ('fifty/ shifty', 'snow-caps/ toecaps', 'lifetime/ unwifed, I'm').

> The track breaks at my toe-caps
>   And drops away in mist.
>   The view does not exist.
>
> Where has it gone, the lifetime?
>   Search me.
>   (*CP*, 195)

These last phrases have all the mannered virtuosity of a 'performance on the Larkin', yet at the same time they are utterly idomatic and commonplace.

Most of Larkin's poems on ageing look back to the past: a past of lost opportunities, or of lost youth. However, in two of his last poems, with an inexorable sense of appropriateness, he turns to look the other way: forward to senility. This is a rare theme in English poetry. 'Heads in the Women's Ward', completed a few months earlier than 'The View' in March 1972, and first published in the atheist journal *New Humanist*, adopts a similar simplicity of idiom to the later poem, but flattened into an unresonant, diagrammatic plainness. The unflinching picture of senility in this poem seems to risk the 'Rationalist Press sunlessness' (*RW*, 157) which Larkin condemned in Stevie Smith, though its emotional distress is perhaps too intense for such a description. Its tone is baldly descriptive ('wild white hair', 'staring eyes', 'bearded mouth'), and its succession of simple tetrameter couplets generates no orchestrated rhetorical climax or witty expression of pessimism. Instead it ends in the gnomic sententious manner of a familiar proverb or epigram:

> Sixty years ago they smiled
> At lover, husband, first-born child.
>
> Smiles are for youth. For old age come
> Death's terror and delirium.
>
> (*CP*, 194)

It is a deliberately disappointing effect, and comes as something of a shock. There is no attempt here to strain, with ironic pathos, after transcendence. The closing banal truisms are crushingly obvious, and the catchy, sing-song rhymes painfully facile.

'The Old Fools', completed in the following year (1973), builds a somewhat more complex rhetorical structure, its register shifting between the loud ill manners of 'This Be The Verse' and the sombre eloquence of 'Dockery and Son'. But its overall effect is as negative and ungratifying as that of 'Heads in the Women's Ward'. The opening tirade crudely assaults the fictions with which we customarily soften the prospect of growing old. The familiar stereotype of the harmless 'old dear' to whom younger people sentimentally condescend is rejected in favour of the equally familiar, but less consoling image of the ridiculous 'old fool' who gets in the way and makes a mess:

> What do they think has happened, the old fools,

To make them like this? Do they somehow suppose
It's more grown-up when your mouth hangs open and
                                                drools,
And you keep on pissing yourself, and can't remember
Who called this morning?

(CP, 196)

The sarcastic tone and 'bad language' have the aggressive attack of
'They fuck you up, your mum and dad'. But in this context the
candour of the poet's iconoclasm is not refreshing, but acutely
painful. It is embarrassingly obvious that this loud ridicule of old
people is an expression of the poet's own displaced terror of death,
which he makes no attempt to hide or transcend. The rudely
insistent, *faux naïf* rhetorical questions (to which there can be no
answers) are a brutally obvious device to bring home the horror of
senility. It is as though the poet has abandoned the decent reticence
of adulthood and reverted to the ingenuous response of a child ('Do
they somehow suppose/ It's more grown-up . . .?') His puzzlement
at the gaga infantalism of the old fools is quite sincere: 'Why aren't
they screaming?'

Only twice does the poem achieve a more emotionally gratifying
poetic register. The meditation on oblivion in the second stanza
briefly modulates into Lawrentian, life-affirming gestures, as the
poet looks back to the past, when life still lay ahead:

It's only oblivion, true:
We had it before, but then it was going to end,
And was all the time merging with a unique endeavour
To bring to bloom the million-petalled flower
Of being here. Next time you can't pretend
There'll be anything else.

(CP, 196)

But the beautiful phrases express only a fleeting nostalgia, a brief
inflexion within the flat, explicit prose: 'Next time you can't
pretend/ There'll be anything else.' Paradoxically, it is the frighten-
ing evocation of the physical state of senility in the third stanza
which contains the most beautiful and evocative imagery in the
poem, though once again the images fail to open out, remaining

157

merely descriptive. A meandering sentence of commas and semi-
colons traces the 'thin continuous dreaming' of senility:

> People you know, yet can't quite name; each looms
> Like a deep loss restored, from known doors turning,
> Setting down a lamp, smiling from a stair, extracting
> A known book from the shelves; or sometimes only
> The rooms themselves, chairs and a fire burning,
> The blown bush at the window, or the sun's
> Faint friendliness on the wall some lonely
> Rain-ceased midsummer evening.
>
> (*CP*, 196–7)

The pondering, meditative mode of Eliot's *Four Quartets* is unmis-
takably echoed here, but with its hints of spiritual insight reduced to
a restless desultory ramble. The images have a bloodless Eliotic
beauty about them ('smiling from a stair', 'The blown bush at the
window'). But there is no redeeming theology in Larkin's version,
only the unbearable pathos of disembodied and fading memories.
The final stanza introduces a potential image of transcendence:
'Extinction's alp'. But any hope of metaphysical, or even of mere
rhetorical, consolation which might be evoked by this traditional
romantic image of the sublime is spoilt. The sublimity of this
summit is only perceptible from a safe distance. For those who are
actually approaching it, it is merely 'rising ground'. They are numb
to its awesome implications.

So flat a denial of emotional or metaphorical consolations is
disconcerting, and critics have sought to evade its implications.
Terry Whalen, for instance, misreads the poem comprehensively,
restoring the consolation which Larkin has so ruthlessly excluded
from it. He reads the ill-mannered tone of the poem's opening as a
dramatised projection of the 'posturing fakery' and 'smugness' of a
young fool. According to Whalen the poem then modulates beyond
this into 'compassion and bewildered reverence' for the 'mysterious
calm' of the old fools (22–3). Larkin's fear of the terror and delirium
of senility becomes, in Whalen's version, a reverence for the serenity
which their delirium so sadly mimics. Against all the expressive
power of Larkin's art this critic manages to detect 'reasons for hope':
'hope, above all, that these lives have accomplished a perfection
which transcends their physical debasement by time'. He goes on to

read the ominous threat of the final words (Well,/ We shall find out') as an invitation to pious philosophising, which 'leaves us pondering the possibilities of meaning' and indicates 'both the value of scepticism and its limitations' (23–4). Margaret Drabble, in contrast, imports no such sentimentalism into the poem, and her reading is truer to its bleak effect. However, she also is reluctant to accept its comfortlessness: 'I read it. I wished I had not. The colour drained out of the sky, a hard grey ashen pall fell over familiar friendly streets, and my fellow passengers [she was on a bus] were transformed into cemetery fodder.' Drabble here gives a new, more uncomfortable, meaning to Larkin's remark that 'A good poem about failure is a success'. Clearly the poem has 'succeeded' in making its effect upon her. But it is a success which she, like many other readers perhaps, finds it difficult to applaud. Drabble is less persuasive when she goes on to defend herself against the discomfort Larkin's poem has caused her by accusing him of 'cowardice': 'He, afraid, wanted us to fear too. He, a coward, wanted us to be cowards too' (62). Here she is mistaken. A poem which robs the sky of its colour may perhaps be 'morbid' or 'unhealthy', but it is difficult to see how it can be cowardly. Cowardice seeks comfort and security. Larkin's poem courageously denies them.

ABSENCE

Though Larkin constantly regrets the impossibility of transcending death, he shows, as we have seen, no interest in transcending life. The greatest intensities of his work derive from his simple, irreducible sense of being alive – 'in the flesh'. When he came to celebrate the city where he spent most of his life, he did not describe the public locality 'Hull', but a private adverbial 'Here', the intimate, unspecific focus of his own temporary presence. Conversely, what most appals him is the thought of his own absence: 'Not to be here,/ Not to be anywhere,/ And soon . . .' (CP, 208). As he said in an interview: 'I dread endless extinction' (RW, 55). Dread however is very close to awe, and Larkin's attitude to absence is full of emotional contradiction. One of his most beautiful poems is entitled 'Absences', and his vocabulary, as has been frequently noted, generates a strange elated catharsis from negative words ('uncontradicting', 'unemphasised', 'unfurnished', 'unaided', 'unnoticed', 'unfenced', 'nowhere'), or apparent negatives ('unfold', 'unclose', 'endless').

A distinction needs to be made here between two kinds of absence in Larkin's work. The first is a simple escape from the pressures and unsatisfactoriness of life. The image of the north ship 'rigged for a long journey' (*CP*, 302) into the ice, for instance, shows an early romantic projection of such an escape. Both the novels end with their protagonists surrendering thankfully to a kind of oblivion. The dream of icebergs and snow to which Katherine surrenders at the end of *A Girl in Winter*, for instance, calms her with its 'implacable' coldness. She is 'in the end glad that such order, such destiny, existed. Against this knowledge, the heart, the will, and all that made for protest, could at last sleep' (248).

Alongside the poetic assertions of 'selfish' liberation which followed the ending of his engagement, Larkin continues to project a contradictory abnegation of self, echoing Katherine's desire to 'sleep'. 'Wants', completed in 1950, for example, expresses a simple yearning to escape the burden of consciousness in the form of a neat elaboration of the commonplace exclamation: 'It's all too much for me'. Its two stanzas reduce the elements of social, sexual and political life to a list of dull phrases reminiscent of early Eliot: 'invitation-cards', 'the printed directions of sex', 'the family . . . under the flagstaff', 'The life insurance'. Life, thus satirically summarised, is enclosed between repeated single lines starkly expressing the desire to escape – first into solitude ('Beyond all this, the wish to be alone'), then, more absolutely, into oblivion:

> Beneath it all, desire of oblivion runs:
> Despite the artful tensions of the calendar,
> The life insurance, the tabled fertility rites,
> The costly aversion of the eyes from death –
> Beneath it all, desire of oblivion runs.
>
> (*CP*, 42)

'Wants' is at bottom a disgruntled antisocial satire. The poet seeks to absent himself from 'the tabled fertility rites' of society through unmarried solitude and ultimately 'oblivion'. The same relatively straightforward desire to escape is perhaps reflected in the mindless 'secret, bestial peace' of 'The Card-Players', completed twenty years later in 1970 (*CP*, 177). Later still a similar oblivion is courted in

'The Winter Palace', completed in November 1978, in which Larkin welcomes his own growing absent-mindedness, in the hope that it will render him oblivious to approaching death – playing extinction at its own game as it were:

> It will be worth it, if in the end I manage
> To blank out whatever it is that is doing the damage.
>
> Then there will be nothing I know.
> My mind will fold into itself, like fields, like snow.
>
> (*CP*, 211)

In other late poems Larkin grimly seeks forgetfulness, like the card-players, in the voluntary soporific of drink: 'I work all day, and get half-drunk at night' (*CP*, 208).

More poetically fruitful, however, is the profounder kind of absence which is projected in 'Absences', completed six months later than 'Wants', also in 1950. This is again an essentially 'escapist' poem; but the rhetoric is quite different. Unusually for Larkin 'Absences' takes an undisguised symbolist form, offering without context or explanation a description of rain falling on a restless sea under a windblown cloudscape. After a beautiful passage of word-painting the final isolated line shifts vertiginously, and without warning to a completely different image:

> A wave drops like a wall: another follows,
> Wilting and scrambling, tirelessly at play
> Where there are no ships and no shallows.
>
> Above the sea, the yet more shoreless day,
> Riddled by wind, trails lit-up galleries:
> They shift to giant ribbing, sift away.
>
> Such attics cleared of me! Such absences!
>
> (*CP*, 49)

The 'oblivion' of 'Wants', and the cynical forgetfulness of 'The Winter Palace', seem sulky and histrionic compared with this larger 'absence'. This is no simple 'oblivion' into which the poet can retreat against the unpleasantness of existence. There is no romantic gesture of rejection here. 'Absences' implies no context of philosophical pessimism or of social satire. Indeed it is devoid of definable emotional design. The description is purely aesthetic and dispassionate. The seascape is awe-inspiring because it has been 'cleared' of the poet's emotional lumber and personal resentments. Its last line is thus an exclamation of both ecstasy and despair. There is no 'desire' for oblivion, no concern with the poet's anxieties, nor even with his death. His 'absence' from this seascape is not part of an emotional strategy; it is a metaphysical fact. As Larkin put it, simply: 'I am always thrilled by the thought of what places look like when I am not there' (*Poet's Choice*, 1962, 202).

The genre to which this poem belongs is a surprising one for Larkin: the sublime ode. Its tones and gestures derive from a long tradition of poems originally designed to celebrate God's presence in nature through a description of an awesome wild landscape. Coleridge's pious 'Hymn Before Sun-rise in the Vale of Chamouni' preserves this original intention. The atheist poet Shelley, on the other hand, contradicting Coleridge, finds no God in Mont Blanc. The waste expanses of his mountain are truly deserted, and their sublimity is a Romantic mystery rather than a lesson in theology. The imaginatively exciting thing about Shelley's mountain is that it is devoid of human presence: 'In the lone glare of day, the snows descend/ Upon that Mountain; none beholds them there.' He concludes that it is not God, but the 'human mind's imaginings' which fill the 'vacancy' created by 'Silence and solitude', and give the landscape its sublimity ('Mont Blanc', 11. 131–44). Like Shelley's landscape Larkin's seascape is sublimely unobserved. But Larkin's ode to Absence goes further than Shelley's. His empty scene fuels no Romantic speculations about the nature of imagination. He is thrilled simply by the fact of his own absence. The poet seeks no transcendence himself. Rather he remains passive while the seascape transcends him. If there is a metaphysical absolute anywhere in Larkin's verse, it is here, in this negative sublime. Larkin understood that in this poem he had succeeded in transforming his selfish 'desire of oblivion' into something more profound. Revealingly he expressed his pleasure in the poem by attributing its composition to another self: 'I fancy it sounds like a different, better poet rather than myself. The last line, for instance, sounds like a slightly-unconvincing translation from a French symbolist. I wish I could write like this more often' (*Poet's Choice*, 1962, 202–3). In this self-less poem he does indeed leave behind the more familiar Larkin of 'Self's the Man' and 'Dockery and Son', wary, defensive, determined to preserve himself from 'dilution'.

This dialectic between the selfish Larkin of 'Wants' and the self-less Larkin of 'Absences' is audible, in less extreme forms, in many other poems. 'Best Society', for instance, probably completed in 1951 but unpublished in the poet's lifetime, shows the 'selfish' Larkin, defending his act of absenting himself from 'society' as necessary to his self-fulfilment. 'Viciously' locking his door against invasion, he welcomes 'Uncontradicting solitude' (defined significantly by a negative adjective). Here his solitude does not lead to oblivion as in 'Wants', but to a kind of tensionless solipsistic paradise similar to that depicted in Andrew Marvell's 'The Garden'. Having aggressively created a space for himself, it seems that he can relax his grip on his tense selfhood. The delicate imagery at the end of the poem suggests a surrender rather than an assertion:

> Uncontradicting solitude
> Supports me on its giant palm;
> And like a sea-anemone
> Or simple snail, there cautiously
> Unfolds, emerges, what I am.
> (*CP*, 56–7)

The word 'Unfolds' here, with its combination of negative prefix and positive connotation, has a characteristic Larkinesque quality. It is as though he cannot risk surrendering himself, as he intensely desires to do, without at least the verbal appearance of scepticism and distrust.

'Long roots moor summer to our side of earth', dated June 1954, and also not published in the poet's lifetime, shows the other, self-less Larkin. It concerns a very specific absence – from Winifred Arnott's wedding. Here, his own refusal to participate in marriage is not selfishly defended. Instead the poet celebrates the wedding, strangely, in terms of his own exclusion from it. Here it is summer, rather than the poet, which delicately 'unfolds':

> It unfolds upward a long breadth, a shine
>
> Wherein all seeds and clouds and winged things
> Employ the many-levelled acreage.
> Absence with absence makes a travelling angle,

And pressure of the sun
In silence sleeps like equiloaded scales.

Where can I turn except away, knowing
Myself outdistanced, out-invented? what
Reply can the vast flowering strike from us,
Unless it be the one
You make today in London: to be married?
(*CP*, 96)

On Winifred's wedding-day his own rejection of marriage seems a refusal to 'flower' or to 'invent'. The burgeoning landscape, described in ecstatic terms reminiscent of Hopkins, has elicited an adequate 'reply' from her, but it excludes and transcends him ('Absence with absence makes a travelling angle'). He can do nothing but 'turn away'.

But Larkin's diction of negative sublimity sounds somewhat forced and out of place here among the emotional and moral problems of his marriage debate. 'Long roots moor summer to our side of earth' is clumsy and unfinished. Far more assured and impressive are the absences and disengagements celebrated in the more generalised context of 'Here', completed in 1961. The poem progresses from detachment into deeper detachment. It begins in the physical separateness of a train, 'swerving' through the landscape. Then it moves to a generalised and dispassionate appraisal of the city's inhabitants: 'residents from raw estates, brought down/ The dead straight miles by stealing flat-faced trolleys . . .// A cut-price crowd, urban yet simple, dwelling/ Where only salesmen and relations come . . .'. The poet remains an observer only, excluded by social fastidiousness from anything but a faintly patronising sympathy with the remote innocence of this 'Pastoral of ships up streets, the slave museum,/ Tattoo-shops, consulates, grim head-scarfed wives . . .' (*CP*, 136).

But it is at the end of the poem, having travelled through the city out into the Holderness peninsula towards the North Sea, that the poet finds the more sublime detachment at which he has been aiming.

Here silence stands
Like heat. Here leaves unnoticed thicken,

Hidden weeds flower, neglected waters quicken,
Luminously-peopled air ascends;
And past the poppies bluish neutral distance
Ends the land suddenly beyond a beach
Of shapes and shingle. Here is unfenced existence:
Facing the sun, untalkative, out of reach.

$\qquad\qquad\qquad\qquad\qquad\qquad$ (*CP*, 136-7)

The repeated prefix 'un-' suggests both a reassuring scepticism and a sublime elation: 'leaves unnoticed', 'unfenced existence . . . untalkative'. To be sure of the greatest emotional effect Larkin leaves unresolved the poet's ambiguous position. Is he secluded, selfishly enjoying the 'unfenced existence' which this landscape affords, safely 'out of reach' of the interference of others? Or alternatively is he excluded, selflessly contemplating an unfenced existence, which is by definition 'out of reach', even of himself? On this second reading the landscape, like the seascape in 'Absences', sublimely transcends the poet.

This kind of analysis might suggest that after all there is a 'religious' element in Larkin's poetry. Responding to Larkin's sublimities J. R. Watson, for instance, insists that 'under the pose is *homo religiosus*, with an awareness of sacred time and sacred place' (358). This is perhaps a question of vocabulary rather than substance. Edna Longley, for instance, also acknowledges the 'hunger' which Larkin is constantly surprising in himself 'to be more serious'; but she defines it as essentially 'agnostic' (78). Certainly the theistic and pious implications of the word 'sacred' seem simply inappropriate to the dispassionate and empty sublimity of these poems. The question may be clarified by reference to that small, frequently overlooked group of pieces within Larkin's *œuvre* which treat natural elements, water, light, air, sun and stars, with a distinctive light-textured lyricism. In 'Water', completed in 1954, for instance, Larkin even jokily invents his own pagan creed:

And I should raise in the east
A glass of water
Where any-angled light
Would congregate endlessly.

$\qquad\qquad\qquad\qquad\qquad\qquad$ (*CP*, 93)

In the place of God his religion places the neatly concentrated and totally unhuman elements of nature, with no spiritual, moral or emotional content, quite unrelated to human values: the free endless play of 'any-angled' light in water. This poem has a strange gravity about it, for all its delicate wit. 'Far Out', completed in 1959, focuses a similarly dispassionate wonder on unnamed distant stars, to whose 'evasive dust' no one looks 'For guidance or delight' (*CP*, 120). More intensely devotional in tone, however, is the imagist poem 'Solar', completed in 1964:

> Suspended lion face
> Spilling at the centre
> Of an unfurnished sky
> How still you stand,
> And how unaided
> Single stalkless flower
> You pour unrecompensed.
>
> (*CP*, 159)

The 'un-' prefixes convey the awesome impersonal generosity of the sun, which requires no human acknowledgement or recognition, 'unaided' and 'unrecompensed' in its 'unfurnished' sky.

> Coined there among
> Lonely horizontals
> You exist openly.
> Our needs hourly
> Climb and return like angels.
> Unclosing like a hand,
> You give for ever.
>
> (*CP*, 159)

The geometrical imagery conveys isolation and exclusion, while in contrast the unclosing hand recalls the welcoming palm of 'Uncontradicting solitude' into which the poet relaxed in 'Best Society'. In some sense this must be allowed to be a 'religious poem'. After all, it takes the unmistakable form of a prayer of supplication, addressed to one of the most universal deities of ancient religion. But this religion is an agnostic one, with no doctrine, no morality, no institutions and no personal god.

It is the stark juxtaposition of such 'religious' imagery as one finds in 'Water' and 'Solar' with the loud gestures of his crude demotic manner which makes the title poem of his final volume, 'High Windows', completed in 1967, one of the most characteristic works of his maturity. The opening of the poem gives no hint of poetic elevation:

> When I see a couple of kids
> And guess he's fucking her and she's
> Taking pills or wearing a diaphragm,
> I know this is paradise
>
> Everyone old has dreamed of all their lives . . .
> (CP, 165)

The poet's exasperation at growing older and his envy of youth leads him into a sulky admission that quite probably 'forty years back' his pious elders similarly envied his own freedom from religious guilt (*'That'll be the life;/ No God any more, or sweating in the dark// About hell and that . . .'*). Then suddenly in the midst of this faintly absurd recapitulation of the imagined resentments felt by an earlier generation, he abruptly breaks off, as if impatient with his own aggressive discontent, and modulates without transition into the furthest flung 'key' imaginable:

> And immediately
>
> Rather than words comes the thought of high windows:
> The sun-comprehending glass,
> And beyond it, the deep blue air, that shows
> Nothing, and is nowhere, and is endless.
> (CP, 165)

The 'high windows' here are those of Larkin's top-floor flat in Pearson Park, Hull (Brennan, 29), though the phrase will suggest a church to many readers. If there is religion here, it is like that of 'Water' and 'Solar', a matter of the impersonal elements rather than a personal god.

The poem repeats in more succinct form the pattern of 'Here'. The poet moves from unsatisfactory social exclusion into the absolution of beautiful emptiness. In this poem however the elements of Larkin's negative sublime take even purer forms. The 'deep blue air' of 'High Windows' is more abstract than the 'bluish neutral distance' of the Holderness peninsula, and the air here is not 'Luminously-peopled', even by midges. Rather, it 'shows / Nothing . . .'. Furthermore, the thought of high windows (by a rhetorical fiction) dismisses even the poet's own words ('Rather than words'), nullifying his poetic function. Wordsworth also found 'a sense sublime' in the element of 'blue sky'. But whereas for him this sense was positive, impelling 'All thinking things, all objects of all thought' ('Lines composed a few miles above Tintern Abbey', 11. 95–102), for Larkin it is 'nowhere'. His rhetoric contrives a sublime emotional elevation out of negatives. It is essential to the effect, for instance, that 'endless' comes emphatically last in the sequence of three adjectives. In actual fact there is 'nothing' to be endlessly prolonged and 'nowhere' to prolong it. None the less 'endless' inevitably carries the force of transcendence, of eternity. The poet dispels his sordid and embarrassing social resentments by the extreme expedient of absenting himself rhetorically from the poem. Once again it is the contemplation of his own absence which most thrills him.

BIBLIOGRAPHY

I : WORKS BY LARKIN IN CHRONOLOGICAL ORDER
OF PUBLICATION

Novels

Jill (London: Fortune Press, 1946; London: Faber and Faber, 1975).
A Girl in Winter (London: Faber and Faber, 1947; 1975).

Poems

The North Ship (London: Fortune Press, 1945).
XX Poems (Belfast: Carswells, 1951).
The Less Deceived (Hessle: The Marvell Press, 1955).
The Whitsun Weddings (London: Faber and Faber, 1964).
High Windows (London: Faber and Faber, 1974).
Collected Poems, ed. Anthony Thwaite (London: Faber and Faber, 1988).

Prose

'The writer in his age', *London Magazine*, 4.5 (May 1957), 46–7.
'Betjeman en bloc' (Review of Betjeman's *Collected Poems*), *Listen*, 3 (Spring 1959), 14–22.
Poet's Choice, ed. Paul Engle and Joseph Langland (New York: The Dial Press, 1962), 202–3 ('Absences' with a short comment by Larkin).

'Four conversations', *London Magazine*, n.s. 4.6 (November 1964), 71–7 (interview with Larkin by Ian Hamilton).

'The unsung gold medallist', *The Sunday Times Magazine*, 27 March 1966, 63–5 (interview with Philip Oakes).

All What Jazz: A record diary 1961–68 (London: Faber and Faber, 1970).

Let the Poet Choose, ed. James Gibson (London: Harrap, 1973), 102–4 (short introduction to 'MCMXIV' and 'Send No Money').

Worksheets of 'At Grass', *Phoenix* 11/12: Philip Larkin Issue (1973/4), 91–103.

'A place to write', Foreword to *A Rumoured City: New poets from Hull*, ed. Douglas Dunn (Newcastle upon Tyne: Bloodaxe Books, 1982), 9.

Required Writing: Miscellaneous pieces 1955–82 (London: Faber and Faber, 1983).

Recordings

'Philip Larkin reads *The Less Deceived*', recording, ed. George Hartley (Hessle: Listen Records/ The Marvell Press, 1958).

'Philip Larkin reads and comments on *The Whitsun Weddings*', recording, ed. George Hartley (Hessle: Listen Records/ The Marvell Press, 1965).

'Philip Larkin, *High Windows*: Poems read by the author', recording, ed. Peter Orr (London: Argo, 1974).

Broadcasts

BBC *Monitor* television programme, introduced by John Betjeman, 1964.

BBC Radio programme: 'The bicycle-clipped misanthropist', produced by Alastair Wilson, 1986.

I I : S ECONDARY M ATERIAL

Alvarez, A. (ed.), *The New Poetry* (Harmondsworth: Penguin, 1962).

Amis, Kingsley, *Lucky Jim* (London: Gollancz, 1954).

Amis, Kingsley, 'Oxford and after', in Thwaite 1982, 23–30.

Amis, Kingsley, *Memoirs* (London: Hutchinson, 1991).

Barthes, Roland, *Mythologies*, sel. and trans.: Annette Lavers (London: Paladin, 1973).

Bayley, John, 'Housman and Larkin: Romantic into Parnassian', *Essays in Criticism*, 41.2 (April 1991), 145–59.

Bedient, Calvin, *Eight Contemporary Poets* (London: OUP, 1974).

Belsey, Catherine, *Critical Practice* (London: Methuen, 1980).

Betjeman, John, *Collected Poems*, enlarged edn (London: John Murray, 1973).

Brennan, Maeve M., ' "I Remember, I Remember", 1955–85', in Salwak 1989, 27–37.

Brett, R. L., 'Philip Larkin in Hull', in George Hartley 1988, 100–14.

Brownjohn, Alan, *Philip Larkin* (London: Longman, 1975).

Chambers, Harry (ed.), *Phoenix*, 11/12 (1973/4): Philip Larkin issue.

Chambers, Harry 'Some light views of a serious poem: A footnote to the misreading of Philip Larkin's "Naturally the Foundation will Bear Your Expenses" ', *Phoenix*, 11/12 (1973/4), 110–16.

Clarke, Steve, '"Get out as early as you can": Larkin's sexual politics', in George Hartley 1988, 237–71.

Cookson, Linda, and Bryan Loughrey (eds), *Critical Essays on Philip Larkin: The poems* (London: Longman, 1989).

Day, Roger, *Larkin* (Milton Keynes: Open University Press, 1987).

Drabble, Margaret, 'Philip Larkin', *The Independent Magazine*, 16 March 1991, 62.

Draper, Ronald, 'The positive Larkin', in Cookson and Loughrey 1989, 94–104.

Dyson, Brian (ed.), *The Modern Academic Library: Essays in memory of Philip Larkin* (London: The Library Association, 1989).

Everett, Barbara, 'Philip Larkin: After Symbolism', *Essays in Criticism*, 30.3 (July 1980), 227–42.

Everett, Barbara, 'Larkin and Dockery: The limits of the social', in George Hartley 1988, 140–52.

Everett, Barbara, 'Art and Larkin', in Salwak 1989, 129–39.

Foster, Paul, Trevor Brighton and Patrick Garland, *An Arundel Tomb*, Otter Memorial Paper number 1 (Chichester: Bishop Otter College, 1987).

Goodby, John, '"The Importance of being elsewhere", or "No man is an Ireland": Self, selves and social consensus in the poetry of Philip Larkin', *Critical Survey*, 1.2 (1989), 131–8.

Goode, J., 'The more deceived – a reading of deceptions', in George Hartley 1988, 126–39.

Hartley, George, 'Nothing to be said', in Thwaite 1982, 87–97.

Hartley, George (ed.), *Philip Larkin 1922–1985: A tribute* (London: The Marvell Press, 1988).

Hartley, George, 'New absence', in George Hartley 1988, 1–8.

Hartley, Jean, *Philip Larkin, The Marvell Press and Me* (Manchester: Carcanet, 1989).

Hassan, Salem K., *Philip Larkin and his Contemporaries: An air of authenticity* (Basingstoke: Macmillan, 1988).

Heaney, Seamus, 'Now and in England', *Critical Inquiry*, 3 (Spring 1977), 471–88.

Holderness, Graham, 'Philip Larkin: The limits of experience', in Cookson and Loughrey 1989, 106–14, (1989i).

Holderness, Graham, 'Reading "Deceptions" – a dramatic conversation', *Critical Survey*, 1.2 (1989), 122–9 (1989ii).

Hughes, Noel, 'The young Mr Larkin', in Thwaite 1982, 17–22.

Hughes, Noel, 'Going home with Larkin', *London Magazine*, 29.1/2 (April–May 1989), 115–19.

Jameson, Fredric, *The Political Unconscious* (London: Methuen, 1981).

Kuby, Lolette, *An Uncommon Poet for the Common Man: A study of Philip Larkin's poetry* (The Hague: Mouton, 1974).

Lerner, Laurence, 'Larkin's strategies', *Critical Survey*, 1.2 (1989), 113–21.

Longley, Edna, 'Larkin, Edward Thomas and the tradition', *Phoenix*, 11/12 (1973/4), 63–90.

Mayhew, Henry, *London Labour and the London Poor*, IV, 'Those That Will Not Work' (1862; London: Frank Cass, 1967).

Martin, Bruce, *Philip Larkin* (Boston, Mass.: Twayne, 1978).

Morrison, Blake, *The Movement: English poetry and fiction of the 1950s* (London: Methuen 1986).

Motion, Andrew, *Philip Larkin* (London: Methuen, 1982).

Osborne, John, 'The Hull poets', *Bête Noire*, 2/3 (Spring 1987), 180–204.

Parkinson, R. N., 'To keep our metaphysics warm: A study of "Church Going" by Philip Larkin', *Critical Survey*, 5 (Winter 1971), 224–33.

Paulin, Tom, 'Into the heart of Englishness' (review of Rossen 1989), *Times Literary Supplement*, 20–6 July 1990, 779–80.

Petch, Simon, *The Art of Philip Larkin* (Sydney: Sydney University Press, 1981).

Ricks, Christopher, 'The Whitsun Weddings', *Phoenix*, 11/12 (1973/4), 6–12.

Rossen, Janice, *Philip Larkin: His life's work* (Hemel Hempstead: Harvester Wheatsheaf, 1989).

Salwak, Dale (ed.), *Philip Larkin: The man and his work* (London: Macmillan, 1989).

Simpson, Matt, 'Never such innocence – a reading of Larkin's "Sunny Prestatyn" ', *Critical Survey*, 1.2 (1989), 176–81.

Skinner, John, 'Philip Larkin by Philip Larkin', *Ariel*, 20.1 (January 1989), 77–95.

Tallis, Raymond, *In Defence of Realism* (London: Arnold, 1988).

Thwaite, Anthony (ed.), *Larkin at Sixty* (London: Faber and Faber, 1982).

Timms, David, *Philip Larkin* (Edinburgh: Oliver and Boyd, 1973).

Timms, David, '"Church Going" revisited: "The Building" and the notion of development in Larkin's poetry', *Phoenix*, 11/12, (1973/4), 13–26 (1973/4i).

Timms, David, 'Philip Larkin's novels', *Phoenix*, 11/12 (1973/4), 153–72 (1973/4ii).

Tomlinson, Charles, 'The middlebrow muse' (review of *New Lines*, ed. Robert Conquest), *Essays in Criticism*, 7 (January 1957), 208–17.

Wain, John, 'Engagement or withdrawal? Some notes on the work of Philip Larkin', *Critical Quarterly*, 6 (Summer 1964), 167–78.

Watson, J. R., 'The other Larkin', *Critical Quarterly*, 17.4 (Winter 1975), 347–60.

Watt, R. J. C., '"Scragged by embryo-Leavises": Larkin reading his poems', *Critical Survey*, 1.2 (1989), 172–5.

Whalen, Terry, *Philip Larkin and English Poetry* (London: Macmillan, 1986; reprinted with alterations 1990).

INDEX